GO WITH WHAT YOU GOT

BARRY SPANIER

Dear Mom

THE
BARE
CHRONICLES

BARRY SPANIER

BARRY SPANIER

Published and distributed by Kaimana Trust, PO Box 82, South Fremantle, WA Australia 6162.

First Edition July 2009 Printed in USA
Second Edition December 2009 Printed in USA

Printed by Maple-Vail Book Manufacturing Group
Book cover design by Mike Coker, Quiqcorp, www.quipcorp.com
ISBN 978-0-9806779-0-4

For Cornelia Spanier,

Thank you for your
boundless love and support.

BARRY SPANIER

Dear mom

THE BARE CHRONICLES

Acknowledgements 8
Up Front 13
The Decision to Build a Boat 19
The Rules 27
The Journey Begins 29
Life Onboard in Maui 51
Maui to Tahiti 71
Bernard Moitessier 81
Tahiti 89
New Zealand 127
The *Constellation* 145
The *Con* Installation 153
Shipwreck 173
Tahiti to Maui 229
Maui 235
My Mom 242
The Sea 244
About the Author 270

RECIPES

Traditional Christmas Eve Seafood Stew 33
Claudette's Meatless Chili 49
Barry's Shrimp Extraordinaire 66
Jamaican Port Tenderloin 90
Chili Rubbed Ahi with Fresh Mango Salsa 106
Birthday Scallops 111
Barry's Salmon With Persimmon Honey & Kombu Glaze ... 133
Wouldn't Whip No More Beets 138
Smoked Oyster Spaghetti *Alfa Centauri* 162-163
Good Chow 166
Squid Ink Pasta & Baked Ahi with Shrimp & Mushroom 240

APPENDIX

Commercial Sail Associates 247

ACKNOWLEDGMENTS

Claudette Haener is at the top of the list because without her constant enthusiasm, support and cooperation, the *Seminole* would probably never have been a reality. Her love and affection are always a part of me.

Hank Jotz gave me skills and knowledge, and encouraged a philosophy that would serve me through a lifetime.

Michael Richardson and *Peter Minkwitz* partnered in the original madness to be floating. **Big Mike, Red**, and **Whompus** kept the boat yard lively, fun, and taught us much about life and practical things to do with boats.

Paul Mitchell was the partner we needed to create **Sail Services** and move on. He just finished a twenty five year circumnavigation.

Emilano Marino (aka *Malcolm Whenke*) and *Robin Lincoln* added the extra energy to help get *Seminole* on the road.

Ken 'Crow' Kaufman was the catalyst for many adventures and helped build out the San Diego loft.

Harlow Dougherty sought me out and drove the voyage onward with his faith in me.

Jamie and Jacque Spence introduced us to dedicated altruism with their *Canvasback* project.

Peter Jones trusted and helped in so many ways and made the Lahaina experience easy to manage.

Patrick Humbert shared everything and loved the *Seminole* as much as I did.

Amber Shock was there to inspire me to be free and find the power.

ACKNOWLEDGMENTS

Joel House and *Moea Sylvain* opened the doors in Tahiti and offered space and peace.

Bernard Moitessier always responded to my letters to keep the dream alive and then became a friend.

David and Anthea Oliphant helped us in our time of need and contributed immeasurably to our survival.

Tony Sheppard brought the Kiwi spirit to our rescue and always had a smile and a good joke to keep things in perspective.

Geoffrey Bourne deserves the major credit for standing with me and growing **MauiSails** through the years, and keeping me from giving it all away.

Lena Kerr-Grant took a chance and survived to start a new life in a new land and was always part of the good things that happened.

Iris Macia-Rose. Sweet Isis, you lived it all and always had a port in the storm. You will be part of the "Rocks" crew forever and each year we salute you with a toast. You passed much too early.

Charles Priester helped us to get home and opened his heart and mind to appreciate my madness.

Cornelia Spanier always believed in me. I could never have done any of it without her constant love and support.

Samantha Spanier saw the vision of this book and pursued it, ignoring my reasoning of why anyone would want to buy it.

Thank you all for helping to make my life joyous, loving, and successful.

Aloha,

Barry

BARRY SPANIER

Why are the thousand streams of dreams so unstoppable?

In these fleeing moments of release,

when I know the peace of all time is always at hand,

there is no need to be concerned.

Lake Merced 1961

UP FRONT

Barry Spanier has been associated with innovation and development in the world of windsurfing and sailing for over thirty years. Currently, he is living and working on his home island of Maui, Hawaii, serving as the Head Sail Designer for **MauiSails**, an internationally recognized competition group.

As an accomplished boat builder and ocean navigator, he spent several years cruising the Pacific on a thirty-eight foot vessel of his adapted design and construction, and counts those vagabond times as some of the best of his life. From those years come wonderful stories of adventures, exotic locations, remote cultures, and even shipwreck tragedy.

IT BEGAN IN 1957

From the time Barry was eleven years old, he dreamt about boats and sailing. Once given the chance to go sailing on a thirty-six foot boat on San Francisco Bay, he luckily became a regular crew member. The weekend outings during the spring and summer months brought the sailing life to the forefront and it sucked him in.

He bought his own eight-foot pram, an El Toro, and quickly became a member of the Lake Merced Sailing Club, spending hours sailing alone on the lake, always devising new rigging, thinking about sails and how it all worked. Sailing became his sport, his dream, and it absorbed him every spare minute.

After years of high level competition, time in college with term papers and studying displaced the racing. The lake was far away, and his dreams had less meaning.

Tioga Pass 1967, photo by Bruce Mabel

But the sixties had a way with Barry's generation. After four years of university and no degree, he dropped out to try another way in the world. There was no plan, but he knew his path at the time wasn't working.

Shortly after, local sailmaker, Hank Jotz, offered Barry a job and he couldn't say "YES!" fast enough. Barry spent a lot of time on his hands and knees doing simple hand work, or learning how to use the machines by sewing sail bags. It was an apprenticeship of instruction and practice, and included Hank's special approach to sailmaking and life in general. Everything he did was always aimed at keeping things simple and making it work. Building sail corners from rope and thimbles, hand sewing rope, hand sewing seams, and all the traditional methods of attaching the sails to the wires were being passed on. Hank didn't like modern solutions so Barry got a decent background in the 'old ways' which has served him well. He was constantly reading and dreaming about ocean sailing, walking the harbors in his spare time, looking for the 'great deal' on a fixer upper boat that could cross oceans.

IT WAS A BIT CRAZY TO ATTEMPT TO BUILD A BOAT OF THAT SIZE WITH NO MONEY. He was twenty-two and his wife, Claudette, twenty, when they lived in Sausalito Harbor on board the fifty-eight foot Peterson schooner, *Fairweather*, for six months. After that, they moved to the Sunset District and lived in a tiny apartment, working full time jobs at three dollars an hour. They saved about two thousand dollars to start their boat project. Youthful enthusiasm and total optimism over-rode their reason. They decided to buy the plans for an Atkins "Ingrid", a thirty-eight foot double-ender, for thirty-four dollars from **Motor Boating Magazine**. There was a new, cheap and easy boat building method called ferro-cement. It looked simple, and they decided to try it. It was a bit crazy to attempt to build a boat of that size with no money. It was 1969.

A plot of land at Pier 62 (at Third and China Basin Street, next to the drawbridge) was rented for thirty-six dollars a month from the San Francisco Port Authority, and in conjunction with two other guys, Barry and Claudette became boat builders. When their truck, and only transport, was wrecked, they rode bicycles across town to their full time jobs, and then peddled to the boat and back across town to go home.

To make life easier and be able to work full time and still put in maximum time on the boat, they moved to the yard where it was being built. An 8'x8'x8' shipping container with the big latch doors became their home for the next three years. It had a peaked roof of used plywood, a pot belly wood burning stove, two pipe cots, a Coleman cooker, and an old porthole. When it got too cramped in the shack, there was an abandoned restaurant where they could bathe in the big sinks and hang out in the booths.

Home Sweet Home in the background

After launching in 1973, the cutter *Seminole* went into a slip at the Golden Gate Yacht Club docks where they would finish the rig, which meant building a sixty foot hollow spruce mast, and boom, with all the hardware, ready for sail.

And sail they did. After a couple months and a few nice afternoons on the Bay, they decided to leave San Francisco on a crisp November day. With Hank Jotz, Mark Heckman, Claudette and Barry aboard, the *Seminole* sailed under the Golden Gate Bridge for San Diego. There the couple founded a small company called **Sail Services**, making yacht sails for a year while completing their cruising preparations. With no fanfare they sold out to partner Paul Mitchell, packed their tools, a sewing machine, some materials, and headed for Mexico.

Photo by Bruce Mabel

Their first on-boat sail repair service came in Puerto Vallarta, where they met a pair of cruising Canadians in self-built fifty footers. Their names were Doug Barron and Rod Knight, and they wanted awnings made for both boats (they had all the materials). The *Seminole* had everything else. Anchored at Punta de Mida and rafted up, their two boats used their generators together to make the electricity needed to run the sewing machine and create the awnings. Staying out there for three days, they would work some, and surf some more.

When the awnings were completed the Canadians asked if they could radio some friends about the sail repair service. Soon there was a parade of sailboats coming out to anchor and hand over their sails for repair. Barry and Claudette made several hundred dollars extra and everyone was happy.

Thus began the onboard sailmaking experiment that supported their adventure across the Pacific.

Barry has a passion for writing, which extends to screenplays, short stories, and poems. While sailing the South Pacific, he chronicled his adventures with letters to his mother, Cornelia Spanier. Fortunately, she kept all of his letters and drawings, which she recently gave him, providing the basis for **The Bare Chronicles**.

Barry will captivate you, challenge you, make you laugh and leave you wondering even more – just who is Barry Spanier?

Samantha Spanier

*Always have ten cents more
than you need to spend.*

Photo by Bruce Mabel

The decision to build a boat came in a moment of reality suspension. Surely, no one who built one before would be as easy to convince, and there was no one to warn us off. It all seemed so simple. Thirty four dollars for the plans, split three ways, and away we went.

Michael Richardson, who looked like a young Groucho Marx, and his friend, Peter Minkwitz, were the partners in this plan. Peter had recently graduated from Berkeley, I was a dropout, and Michael was running from the draft board. If we pooled tools and resources, bought materials in bulk, we thought we could each make a cheaper boat. It was not quite a commune since we would build three boats, but what did we know? Some experience sailing small boats, some reading about the voyages of others, and plenty of dreaming was enough to make us look beyond the obvious fears of failure.

Building *Seminole* was a youthful dream, a project worthy of its own story. The years we would spend in the grimy boatyard and living in the container would be filled with lessons in friendship, cooperation, universal blessings, and rewards for risks taken.

The first months were spent lofting, making station molds, and scrounging the materials to build strongbacks and the rest of the structure that would be removed after the hull was plastered. Fortunately, the area where we had the yard was a major shipping terminal and there were huge piles of useable timber everywhere. It came onto the pier as dunnage; plywood, 2 x 10's, and pallets. We made friends with longshoremen who arranged truckloads to be delivered for free. We used fifty-five gallon drums filled with water to form the foundation for the wood which defined the shape of the boat.

Ferro-cement is not a particularly fun material to work with in a refined shape. It begins with four layers of chicken wire over your form, followed

Photo by Bruce Mabel

by quarter-inch diameter garage-door spring wire on two-inch centers horizontally, three-sixteenths rod on two-inch centers vertically, making a square pattern. Then you cover that with four more layers of mesh, the outside one being three-eighths. This forms a matrix of wire you have to tie tightly together. For months, Claudette and I would work, she on the outside dropping U-shaped pieces of wire at the intersections of the rods, me on the inside using aircraft pliers to twist it tight.

When every intersection was secured the hull already had a solid feel. It was a wire cage about three-quarters of an inch thick, fair and smooth in lamplight. Our hands were scarred, and generally scratched and bloody from the many encounters with sharp little wire ends everywhere. We worked our day jobs, and then worked on the boat as late as we could stand to be out in the cold, before cleaning up our tools and getting to bed.

Plastering was a one day operation, well planned and executed with lots of help from about twenty friends. Big work lights showed up donated by the tugboat crew nearby, and food came from the boat yard families. We started mixing the custom mortar about two in the morning and finished about midnight. That was only the beginning.

Curing took about a month, so we worked on building deck beams and other structural parts that needed to be laminated. Surface preparation and painting sealed and protected her, and then we had to figure out how to roll her over. We called it "Egyptian Engineering". Big wheels were made of dunnage lumber with steel plates bolting them together. A strap made of flat metal was fastened along the entire edge like a wagon wheel. Using wheels from the heavy longshore carts, a giant rolling machine with huge blocks and ropes was fashioned. This is where the Egyptian thing came from. It took several days of preparation, jacking and shifting to get the boat hanging in the giant wheels, and a whole day to roll her upright. No crane or heavy equipment to pay for, plus some ingenuity, persistent work, and brute strength saved thousands of dollars.

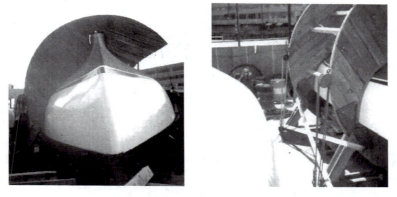

With the boat in her cradle we quickly built a roof over the entire deck with salvaged lumber and plywood from old shipping crates. This allowed work on the structural floors rain or shine, as well as pouring concrete and steel balls for the ballast, building water tanks in the keel, and constructing the cabin sole. Major bulkheads were cut, fitted, and glued to the webs we had in the hull structure, and soon there was a workbench and bed frame. We were now living aboard. It was winter.

On sunny days we would pull off the temporary roof and be outside fitting beams and building the core structure of the decks. When we burned out from too many weeks of non-stop work till midnight, we would take a bottle of Port wine and wander the harbors looking at boats. If we were lucky, we would

run across folks like Al and Marjory Peterson on *Stornaway*, or other souls who were committed to life on the sea, which inspired us to keep going.

Building a boat is about endless tasks of repetition. Thousands of screws followed by the plugs to fill the holes, along with through-bolts, carefully fitted wood joints, all repeated in steady similarity, yet each one its own task. A meditation for sure.

Months turned to years. The boat yard became so familiar, and the people who frequented the place became solid friends. There was a crew of old guys who would sit and give good natured advice and the crazy guy who hit himself. And there was the stream of other boat builders who would cruise by looking for inspiration of their own, often stopping with a six-pack or a gallon of cheap red to talk until the bottles were empty.

All the woodwork began to demand more and more care as we shifted into the finish phase. Now we were working with teak and other high end woods. We managed to find black locust for the threshold treads, ironwood for the bits and rub rails, and fine Port Orford cedar for the cabin sides. As the

Barry in blacksmith shop. Photo by Steve Wilkings

cabin structures grew finished, whenever there wasn't good weather to work outside we were roughing out the interior cabintry and furniture. It was just plywood. Someday it could be better.

I made patterns for all the bronze hardware, and arranged casting and machining. Local blacksmith, Tony Roselleni at Edwin Klockars Toolmaker, provided the answer to getting all the ironwork done. Tony and I agreed I would work four hours for him and then I could work four hours on my stuff. This way I was able to make the engine beds, chain plates, bowsprit fittings, all the mast hardware, boom gallows, and anything else that required forming or welding in metal.

Before the cockpit went in we laid in the two-cylinder diesel, fuel tanks and exhaust system. There were portholes to install, hatches to build, winch islands to construct from fibreglass, and hardware to position all over the deck. The bowsprit and boomkin finished the deck spars and lifelines and pulpits followed, but there would be no electrical system or major plumbing.

In late October of 1973, after almost four years of life at Pier 62, we had only the rudder to finish and we could launch. The interior was still bare plywood and had no finish except the cabin structure. It was like a mockup of the inside except it had already become our home for a good while. Getting in the water was going to be so fine... no more climbing up and down the scaffold and no more Third Street traffic noise and dirt. The night before the crane was to come and drop us in, we sat in the little container shack with a good friend who came by knowing we were getting ready to launch. It was raining so hard little waterfalls were pouring out of the scupper holes in the toe rails. But we knew it would be fine for our day. And it was.

Floating is way better than living in a boatyard. We had a slip and could live like real people again. The only drawback was the slip's location in the harbor on the City Front. Our dock was almost out in the bay, so when the weather turned bad, we had lots of line tending to do to keep the boat off the pilings as the tides changed. But floating was still preferable.

During this short period we built the mast, boom, spreaders, and got all the rigging ready for stepping the mast. Building the mast was a killer task because we had to build a sixty-five foot gluing bench along one wall of the loft. Long threaded rods with fender washers would serve to put the pressure on when the eight by twelve inch box was glued. I remember it taking several months to execute. What a pleasure it was to run the big hand plane down the edges and peel paper thin coils of spruce.

The gluing was done by four of us and after the months of getting it all ready, only a few hours of work would make it or break it.

Once the mast was secured in the boat we finished the running gear, winch installations, etc., and began the sails. We were happy to work late into the night to get that part done because it meant sailing was the next step. The first sail would be like an exhalation, a huge reward after years of sacrifice and hard work.

The first day went perfectly. It is impossible to say how amazing it was to raise the sails and feel the first surge of natural power as we shut down the diesel and got into silent mode. The Golden Gate Bridge was our first goal. We sailed under it and had a moment to think about what we had done, just the two of us. The day was cold and gray, but it took nothing away from the deep sense of accomplishment and anticipation of sailing out the Gate again soon, turning left, and not looking back.

A few long sessions in the loft got us all the sail covers, deck canvas of all kinds, and final interior touches for making a trip. We were ready to go south. It was a simple decision to leave and to do it without much talk. We loaded up everything we owned that wasn't already onboard, and five days later we were in San Diego looking for a new life.

The exterior of the *Seminole* looked as good as any well built yacht of the era. She was hardly recognizable as a 'cement' boat. One day I was looking for a job as a shipwright at Kettenburg yard and told the foreman I would bring the boat around so he could see a sample of what I could do, especially since almost every detail was done by either Claudette or myself. He came aboard and while Claude made tea we sat down below and talked for about twenty minutes. I could see him eyeing every joint and finish of what was actually completed. He asked me what she was planked with, implying he was in a wooden boat. I think when I replied, "Portland #5", he was offended to have been fooled. I got no offer of a job.

We eventually found a great slip in a tiny set of docks behind Carl Eichenlaubs' boatyard. It was right next door to the Red Sails Inn and just another door away from our new loft above San Diego Marine Supply. We could walk from our work to our boat in two minutes and would spend the next year creating the business called **Sail Services**, making dozens of new friends in the cruising and boat building community, as well as finishing more of the voyaging gear. A wind vane for self steering, full bow to stern awnings for sun protection at anchor, man-overboard gear, and well organized food storage rounded out the preparation. Meanwhile, there was still no electrical system or head. We were dependent on kerosene lamps for

down below and running lights. A good quality heavy duty bucket in a hole of the foc'sle functioned perfectly every time in lieu of the dreaded marine toilet.

That year went by so fast, we hardly had time to think about what was next. As well as finishing the boat, **Sail Services** was rapidly growing, both business-wise and socially. We conducted weekly classes in sail repair and maintenance, and every Thursday evening was dedicated to accoustic music night with the Moron Block and Tackle Choir, led by Malcolm Whenke.

In spite of all the fun and success we were having, we knew we wanted to keep going and not get hung up working again. So with less noise than we made leaving San Francisco, we simply packed up some materials, tools, and a favorite sewing machine and got ready to head out. In the dawning light of a late November day in 1975, my faithful partner, Paul Mitchell, came to the dock and slipped a thousand dollars in my pocket and said, "Have a good time." The business was his, we were on our way. The next chapter was about to be written.

8.   DON'T DO DUMB THINGS

1.   DON'T COP TO A THING

2.   SNOOZE YOU LOOSE

3.   TIGHT IS RIGHT

4.   DON'T GIVE CHAFE A CHANCE

5.   DON'T LET YOUR DEAL GO DOWN

6.   KEEP 7 UP

7.   STANDARDS

THE RULES
FROM THE LOFT WALL
SAIL SERVICES, SAN DIEGO 1975

THE JOURNEY BEGINS

*If you hold on to the dream and work towards it,
someday it will really happen.*

November – December 1975
San Francisco – Puerto Vallarta

We arrived in Mexico and cleared all the various agencies in Cabo San Lucas, a charming little fishing village that was beginning to see a growth in Norte Americano tourism. It had wonderful good vibes and we felt safe in the anchorage.

The trip down, though, was a wild ride for several days. Almost as soon as we left, the wind became very strong and *Seminole* had her first test as far as sea keeping goes. We had Malcom Whenke and Robin Lincoln on board as crew and voyaging partners and this certainly helped to ease the

burden for Claude and I. The only sad part was Malcom's constant seasickness. The poor guy was such a green color most of the time, it looked un-natural and he rarely ate for the whole trip.

When we were twenty-four hours into the passage, the wind was in a thirty-to-forty knot range with huge following seas. We were well offshore though and felt very safe since *Seminole* handled it with such grace. During one period of several hours, I sat out on the sprit pulpit and watched while the steering vane held her perfectly on course with just a small stays'l and triple reefed main. It seemed really wild at the time to be leaving her to steer herself, but after seeing it work successfully for hours on end, I never again doubted the setup.

As the days rolled by with no serious problems, we gained experience and confidence with the boat. We decided to try to go into Magdalena Bay as we had heard about this area as a good place for a stop. On a nice clear morning we had the **Sailing Directions** out, and were doing our best to figure out where we might be, based on the indistinguishable coastline of brown and tan rocks and sand. We were merrily sailing in this opening, thinking we were doing fine, when suddenly the bottom started coming up at us,

31

shoaling into little breaking waves all around. Between us, we managed to figure out we had taken a wrong turn somewhere and were in the wrong place. Fortunately, our voyage didn't end early as we turned her around and aimed straight back offshore again.

Once safely offshore, we decided going all the way to Cabo was best, and we gave up exploring until we were better able to navigate with some certainty. This was not a situation for 'on-the-job training'. Mistakes have a very high cost.

Cabo afforded us the opportunity to find good Mexican meals, wander around in a village atmosphere, and take on water and fresh stores. After a few days, we decided Puerta Vallarta was the best option for Christmas, as we heard P.V. was where the really big party was and it was a very safe harbor situation so we could leave the boat for a few days and not fear. We were interested in Guadalajara and Tepic to do a little touring on land.

The passage to P.V. was kind of scary because of all the heavy commercial ship and ferry traffic, another big lesson for us small boaters. We quickly learned they don't seem to look out for you and 'right-of-way' is meaningless when you are tiny and the other guy is huge and on a schedule. That first night was a real lesson in what to be afraid of and we were really glad when it was over.

TRADITIONAL CHRISTMAS EVE SEAFOOD STEW

The family tradition, but I can't remember whose family. Could have been one of the wives. Could have been my Mom. But traditions don't have to be twenty or thirty years to be a tradition. You're just doing something but don't know why you're doing it. You just had to have seafood stew on Christmas Eve.

1 1/2 cup potatoes cut in small 1/2 inch cubes
4-5 shallots cut up finely – add basil
2-3 cloves garlic – finely chopped
Cook in butter till shallots and potatoes are soft and slightly browned.

Add 1 can cream of celery soup
1 1/2 cup whole milk or some half & half
1/2 cup white wine.
Add clams, shrimp, scallops, crab claws, imitation crab, mussels and any other seafood.

Serves 6 people.

December 27, 1975
Puerto Vallarta

Dear Mom,

This is going to be one of those letters that will probably be passed around. When we first arrived in Mexico we wrote a whole stack of letters in long hand and took them to the post office in Cabo San Lucas to mail them. Airmail seems to be the only way to have any mail arrive at its destination, so to our surprise we found it would cost us about four dollars to mail the first bunch of letters and cards. This is a bit too rich for our very limited cruising budget, so from now on we'll just write one or two long letters to persons who will then see that everyone gets to read them. This is really the only way we can do it. We would love to be able to correspond with everyone, but it is almost impossible.

Puerto Vallarta is pretty much done as the quaint little Mexican fishing village. It's now a market for the grand collection of junk very well hidden beneath this flashy exterior. The people largely understand English, though not speaking it too well, and they are friendly and helpful. Markets for fruits and vegetables are clean and orderly and the fruit is all tree ripened and delicious. Has anyone ever held a papaya weighing twelve or fourteen pounds and as big as a watermelon? Avocados that weigh four pounds apiece? And both for about twenty cents a pound. Not much on crispy vegetables, so salads have to be made with cabbage and beet greens and the like. The lettuce is too dangerous to eat, being a prime source along with tomatoes, of the dread Mexican trots. Malcolm, one of our crew, is presently afflicted with this malaise as a result of a day of culinary adventures in town. It is a persistent and very troublesome disease, possibly curable only through drastic measures. Many other cruising folks are also suffering and having trouble getting rid of it. Claudette, Robin, and I are having no trouble, but we have been careful about what and where we eat.

The anchorage we're in is very crowded. This was due to the annual Christmas party, and now it's over things are beginning to thin out somewhat. At the peak of it, there were about fifty boats in a very small bay, so your neighbor was generally about twenty or thirty feet from you. If he was the type to run an electric generator all the time or just generally be loud, it was uncomfortable. Also, with that number of boats, the use of dinghies with outboard motors increased almost to a freeway level. One of the things that bugs me the most is those stinky whining outboards. I'm Ok with their use if the distance is great between the shore and the boat (we don't use one ourselves, finding rowing to be good exercise) but here one could practically walk to shore and still they roar about constantly. I'm sure they don't do much for the water, which is already so foul you wouldn't swim in it. Sometimes it is bad enough we hesitate to wash down the decks with it.

Right now, I'm going to settle down and do a moderate sized repair for a small boat in the anchorage. Seems as though he couldn't get his genoa down so it sort of ripped to pieces. After some botched attempts at repair, he came and asked for help. If we could get a couple of these every week we'd have no sweat keeping the kitty status quo. This little job is all that really keeps us in P.V. for the time being. I would say we'll leave here on the 30th for a run into Banderas Bay. All along the shore of the bay, which is about the size of Monterey Bay, there are small fishing villages and Indian towns. They are generally built on or near the rivers which run into the bay and often have fresh water waterfalls. The water where the boat will be anchored is clean and clear with good diving, fishing, and swimming. The anchorages are not as secure though, and often you have to hang on a sandy shelf with a big drop-off very close to the surf line. Still it's better than lying here rotting with the rest of these electrified floating campers. It seems all the places we hear about that are quiet and clean are far away from any sources of fresh water, food, or supplies. This is understandable after seeing the way everyone around us continues to live as though they are still tied up to a marina in the U.S. Ice, booze, meat, eggs, and dairy products, along with being generally suspect of carrying one or more diseases or parasites, are very expensive. This will eat up your cruising budget real fast, as well as tie you to the crowded dirty places. To be able to carry or make these things is also expensive as it takes a toll on the engine (not to mention nerves) charging batteries all the time.

A few days before Christmas we took a side trip to Guadalajara. What a place. The air pollution and general dirt was so bad we simply got back on the train the next morning and returned to P.V. I suppose there

are parts of the town that aren't as bad as the section we were trapped in, but it's difficult to find them without the mobility of good public transportation. We spent the best part of a day in the huge Mercado Libertad and the surrounding city area. It is unfair to condemn the whole city just because we were having trouble breathing, but it made it so we didn't want to stay there any more. The countryside between here and there is unaffected by the blight of the cities except for the ever present plastic bags, containers, and tin cans. All this stuff is strewn about like all the other garbage but it doesn't' go away like the more easily biodegradable items.

Dec 29, 1975

It sure is easy for the days to go by. Yesterday was almost wholly consumed with a navigation discussion in the morning on board a boat with a bonafide navigation instructor as a crewmember, and I completed the repair job I had began the day before. The response from the fellow who wanted the work done was rather disappointing. I offered to do the job as well as instruct him how to effect repairs in the future; we agreed on a price and it wasn't until the job was almost done he hedged on the deal. I think he saw how "easy" it was and figured maybe it wasn't worth it. I agreed to the second price, but from now on I figure to just keep the work to myself. We need the work badly now. I'm sure our funds will last only about three more months if we can't find a job or two along the way. This would make Costa Rica the next logical spot to be able to replenish the pot.

Today, we discovered the water in one of our tanks now tastes like sewage. This water was supposed to be good. We got it in Cabo San Lucas and I'm sure health wise it is OK, but it's unpalatable. This same water was in all the tanks but perhaps the length of time it sat was responsible for the smell and taste. It means removing the inspection ports and getting in and scrubbing them clean, as well as the hauling of more fresh water out to the boat. The water people get here is purified. It is really the only way to be safe from hepatitis and typhoid, and it costs three pesos for five gallons. You can see at that rate, we won't be using it to shower. The city water, which is questionable but free, can be used for bathing, washing dishes and clothes, as long as you are careful with it. It will be some time until we're able to use our rain catchers to fill our tanks as this is the dry season and there will be no rain for about three months. It is sure going to be nice to be in some place where there is fresh water in abundance so we can swim and drink without fear. I think that factor alone may influence us to go to the South Pacific as soon as we leave Costa Rica.

The Royal Viking Star just pulled in this morning and disgorged a load of bandy legs making the town into a sideshow again. Some are more unobtrusive than others, but on the whole they stand out here. I did think of you, Mom, and the trip you took to the Caribbean and figured no matter what, at least those people will go home with some impression of the way others have to live in places that are not as together as the U.S. Even in a place like P.V. the view has to be somewhat of a shock to someone who hasn't ever dealt with the dirt and disorder. It assaults you constantly. Buses are jammed tighter than any "L" Taraval street car ever thought of getting, and are bouncing and lurching on roads that leave a lot to be desired; flies are everywhere on stuff that has been sitting for who knows how long (we stick to only fruit in the skin and peeled vegetables to stay healthy); and babies and pregnant women are everywhere you look. Maybe having seen these things will plant the seeds of change in a few minds so someday it might be different. Sandy Oehmen was right when she said no matter how little we might think we can get by on, it will always be more than these people have had in perhaps a whole lifetime. It makes me very self-conscious about my apparent wealth, especially when you know the guy with the sinking dugout canoe who fishes near the boat in the morning depends on the few fish he may catch with a hand line to make a living. And here we sit, fat, with our yacht and our regular trips to town to buy food, without working. It is pretty conspicuous and sometimes a bit hard to handle, probably the hardest thing to handle. It is really the ultimate degree of shoving someone's face in it. No way around it, we stick out like a sore thumb.

On the brighter side is the upcoming adventure to explore the north side of the bay. We are going to be leaving on the 31st and will probably return in three or four days. When we get back, I'll finish this and mail it.

BARRY SPANIER

We have just returned to the sinkhole of P.V. harbor for the remainder of our stay in Bahia Banderas. While anchored in the most delightful bay off of the town of La Cruz, we were approached by two Canadians who wanted us to build two good-sized awnings and a bunch of other small items before they crossed to the Marquesas. I wouldn't have done it except we really needed the money. For $150, it was worth dragging out the sewing machine. Claude used this time to paint and generally catch up on the little things that were left undone before we left S.D., or the things we discovered along the way, like the baggy wrinkle on the upper shrouds to keep the genoa leech from chafing to death.

Later......our stay in La Cruz was more like what it's supposed to be. Quiet. Peaceful. Clean water to swim and dive in all the time, and a nice beach to explore. A small fishing village with no tourist intrusions and no crowd of other boats in the anchorage. For some reason, it just hasn't been discovered yet. Hope it stays that way for a while.

On New Years Eve the town had a real blowout. It was loud, with everyone hooting and hollering, dogs howling and roosters crowing all night long. This went on until 8.00am under a starry sky, with us on a glassy calm sea. It was something to be able to sit in the dinghy and row around the boat, enjoying the aromas of the village; the cooking for the fiesta, the fish you always smell in these places, and the animals, plus the new and different sounds all around us like some strange symphony. Then to think how many other New Years we had at Pier 62 to be part of the same thing in a dream. It made us realize how important our dreams are and if you hold on to the dream and work towards it, someday it will really happen. Now we have new dreams to follow and many more places that will be new and strange.

When we returned from La Cruz, we were greeted by a huge pile of mail and it was a grand occasion. Letters from all those people who we have shared so many good times with were read again and again, and now will be responded to in order to keep the chain of correspondence going.

Love to all,

Barry & Claudette

January-March 1976
Mexico

Once we left Puerto Vallarta the cruising life began to be more like what we'd imagined. The comfort of the crowd no longer seemed necessary and we were gaining confidence in our boat handling and coastal navigation skills. Heading south along the coast felt perfectly natural. We heard all the stories about safe little bays and small villages and were ready to discover them for ourselves. Malcolm was whole again after his touristas, and nothing was going to hold us back.

We planned all our destinations to be within a day sail to help Malcolm keep weight on his dwindling frame. The little passages also gave us an opportunity to practice celestial navigation and we added that to our coastal plotting to check its accuracy. Further south, the coast became barren and unforgiving except for tiny bays and a few narrow river mouths. The first stop was Bahia Tenacatita, calm and welcoming, surrounded by mangroves and white sandy beaches. If we wanted to eat well we went sailing and fished. Every time we put out hooks we caught fat Spanish mackerel and dined with abandon. We were getting in the groove.

We began to have the chickenskin experiences I knew were waiting in the ocean world. Pods of dolphins chased giant schools of fish, herding and hunting them in a frenzy. At night we would go diving and clouds of phosphorescence would trail off our fins, a wake of stars, glitter skin. The wonderful woman who ran the little restaurant in the palapa by the beach took our dry beans in trade for fixing a killer meal using the fish we caught. Days were spent reading, walking, exploring the mangroves in the dinghy, and just lazing about. Life was slowing down.

One night we moved to a new anchorage and ran into a Brown 31 trimaran, *Sea Spider*, with Jamie and Jacque Spence on board. We had the fish, they had the rest, and we made a great meal together. It turned out they were going to Santiago, near Manzanillo, to get married and hook up with the John Muir family. The Muir family are the people who produced the wonderful spiral bound classic every hippie owned, **The Idiots Guide to**

Volkswagen Maintenance. The Muir family group would be there for a month of meetings and parties and Jamie invited us to become part of it.

The sail was fantastic. Easy and fast, the strong northwesterly carried us in fine style all the way into the bay. We anchored off the Manzanillo commercial harbor and made our way straight to Bar Social, one of the legends in the cruising world we needed to follow up. Rumor had it you could live off the place for the cost of a few beers. They had a 'happy hour' from four to six in the evening where the little plates of delicious seafood and other local treats kept coming as long as you had a beer going. Mariachis, sweaty workers, aging hookers... the place had everything and great food. We felt like successful explorers.

I'M RETIRED AND LIVING OFF MY FORTUNE. After a visit to the huge market to fill the lockers, we were ready to go. The boat was sitting pretty about a hundred yards from the fishing boat pier and I was lounging around waiting for the others to come back from their shopping missions. Grubby would have been complimentary, with my long hair, sombrero, and homemade clothes.

It was hot and dry. The pier smelled of diesel and dead fish. A white shoed foot tapped mine and I looked up to see a caricature of a middle aged American standing there. The shoes, cranberry pants, a cream colored jacket, gold chains, and CIA sunglasses. He started by asking if I knew anything about the day charter rates and schedules. We talked about fishing a bit, then he said, "What are you doing here?"

I said "That's my yacht out there, and I'm waiting for my crew."

He looked a little stunned. After a pause, he said, "How did someone like you get a boat like that?"

I had to rub it in. "I'm retired and living off my fortune." That actually drove him off. He never said a word. I just went back under the sombrero until the crew came back.

After a sail across the bay, we anchored in a little man-made cove in front of the Las Hadas Resort, unfinished yet, and said to have already cost one-hundred ten million dollars. A Bolivian tin billionaire named Betino created it for his jet setting friends, but no one came to the party. It was empty. It was great for us though because they were happy to have yachts anchored in the picture perfect bay, and to have people to use the facilities. A billionaire's dream right off our front porch. We were really laughing.

Several weeks passed in that bay, most of them anchored on the other side of the little peninsula from Las Hadas, near the hacienda where the Muir people were living. We got in on the Spence wedding, with lots of crazy partying, and had enough fun for normal people to have in ten years, all crammed into those short hours.

Next came Ixtapa, a shallow bay, well protected, with fantastic diving that made the perfect pit stop before heading into magical Zihautenejo. There is only room for a few boats so we luckily made it there alone and took the center ground for a couple of days.

WE BEGAN TO HAVE THE CHICKENSKIN EXPERIENCES I KNEW WERE WAITING IN THE OCEAN WORLD.

More diving and fishing kept us eating well and totally happy to be alive. Our past lives were getting farther and farther behind us now. We did yoga on the beach, swam to and from the boat every morning, caught up on maintenance, and generally enjoyed the silence and nature of the place. From what I understand now, there are numerous hotel towers and condos and the quiet little place is no more.

The Zihuatenejo festival was a highlight. Noisy, a bit drunken, but totally friendly and inclusive, it was a party like we'd never seen before. We made friends fast and those new acquaintances brought us to new adventures in waterfalls and jungle exploration.

One night Malcolm heard noises while in his stern cabin birth. He crept forward through the engine room and woke us up, and I got the machete from the foc'sl. It was an odd sound and he didn't really know what it was, so we crept slowly along the deck to the stern. When we looked over the side, there was a very drunk guy hanging onto the rudder, and hiccupping. We were cautious but realized the guy was just worn out and taking a rest. Malcolm's Spanish was good enough for him to figure out our intruder was there because he had fallen asleep on the beach drunk and missed his ride with the other crew members. When he woke up he decided to swim to his shrimp boat.

We got the dinghy together and rowed the guy home. He was very grateful and apologetic. The next day we were visited by his boat crew who gave us a big bucket of fat shrimps and invited us over for a fiesta later that day. What a grand party it was too. Guitar music, lots of marijuana (they use it for seasickness), beer and tequila, and plenty more shrimps and fish to eat. The guys on that boat became best friends in the anchorage for the rest of our stay.

The next short passage took us to Acapulco. The plan was to find work at the yacht club so we could afford provisions for the rest of the trip to Costa Rica. We'd developed many friendships and connections and we already knew of several boats interested in having awnings and covers made. It was easy to lay anchored off the club, use the deck of one of the customers, a fifty-foot power yacht, and set up shop. With the cash from the work, trips to the supermarket in town were made regularly and soon the *Seminole* was filled with new canned goods and grains.

Robin and Malcolm decided to make their own way from this point and eventually ended up in Costa Rica. But Claudette thought she was pregnant so we decided to go to Hawaii for the baby to be born in the U.S. (As it turned out, she wasn't.) In retrospect we must have been totally stupid or insane, but we got ready to go, did a lot of practice navigation, and finally just slipped away one morning without any real good-byes.

A letter from Claudette

April 18, 1976
Mexico to Maui

Dear Mom and Dad,

It is Easter Sunday and I'm thinking about you and wondering how you are spending the day. We are almost six hundred miles off the Mexican coast. We have been out a week now, leaving Manzanillo April 11. I'd say we are doing real good. It has been overcast the last few days and we are certainly looking forward to the trade winds. Wind is pretty fluky here. It goes from light to strong to light winds. That is rather frustrating since the vane won't steer us under those conditions AND we have to sit there at the helm hour after hour. We finally "hove to", (lashed the helm, backed the staysail) and went to sleep. We opened up one of our two bottles of Vin Rose today and it sure did taste good.

April 25

Well, another week has gone by and we are in the Northeast trades. We have been making at least 100 miles a day and by tomorrow evening we will pass the half way point. Right now it is a little uncomfortable because the seas are on our beam and it makes it quite rolly. Hopefully a few more degrees of longitude will make the seas much better. This rolling and lurching is for the birds. It makes cooking a real endurance test. Things slide and fly off the counter and get dumped. So far pancake batter and soup have gotten away from us and what a mess to clean up. We keep our sense of humor right up there though, and when that fails we talk about a farm in Oregon or a new boat. Then it can get so good we talk about going on in this boat. Before that though, we would have to do some changes.

What we need most is a Tiller Master. It is an auto pilot that uses electricity (so we would have to put in an electrical system) and it will steer the boat when the wind is light or when we are using the engine. The other thing we need is a dodger. This will go over the main hatch and the cockpit like a windshield to protect us from the wind, spray and rain. We will also put in electric running lights and a light over the chart table. Kerosene is a real mess. It usually runs over and all down your arm and on the floor, and then half the time, the lights blow out. The stove goes too, propane next time. It runs on kerosene too, and trying to fill it when the boat is rolling isn't a fun job. We will re-do the galley so that there are two sinks and the counter goes straight across and a little lower.

So, you see we have lots to do, but we still want to enjoy our stay in Maui. It will be well earned by the time we get there. We are both anxious for a meal out, cold beer, ice cream, and I really want a grilled cheese sandwich. Not to mention an eight hour sleep and a hot bath would sure feel good. Ah, the little things one takes for granted. But we have our rewards too. The sky is full of a billion stars. We saw a rainbow this morning and the sea is a blue that I didn't know existed, and the sun is a warm friend. The last six hundred miles will be the best sailing. Meanwhile *Seminole* pushes on for that quiet anchorage in a new land, with new foods, new people. It is exciting to look forward to.

April 29

Getting closer everyday. The seas are on our stern, which makes the motion real comfortable. We've been eating more interesting food now that it is easier to prepare. We are sailing downwind and both the headsails are set out on poles. Though there isn't much wind we are going forward. The wind is supposed to be blowing from the Northeast but last night it swung around to the Southeast. The wind is so light that we could walk faster, but we are having a good time and there isn't that much of a hurry. Today we took baths and washed our hair. It felt good to get clean. It is wonderful the way salt water is so refreshing. When it is nice like this you forget what it was like when it was uncomfortable. Today I got the water colors out that I bought in Manzanillo and tried some painting. Results were a little out of proportion but it was fun. Maybe someday I'll take an art class. There are so many things to do besides sail. I know someday I want some land so we can grow flowers and have fruit trees and a vegetable garden, a few cats and dogs, a litter of pigs, etc.

May 2

Another Sunday. We caught a fish this morning, a good sized dorado. They are a beautiful fish, bright yellow when in the water and as they die, they turn dark blue. Makes me feel bad to kill them but we really wanted something fresh to eat. Cooked up some brown rice and steamed the fish, with soy sauce, it tasted great. We ate it for lunch too, and tonight is spaghetti. The wind has picked up again. Sure am glad as the last few days it has been real slow. With twelve hundred miles in front of us, and only making one and a half miles an hour, I was feeling sort of low. Figured out there had to be a reason. I picked up the Christian Science Sentinel and there right off was an article on "What's the hurry, you always are where you belong." It made me start thinking and I realized that all the times I wished I had more time for myself to read, write, draw and now that I have it after two and a half weeks, I'm tired of it. Well, I kept reading since it was making me feel better, went to sleep, and when I woke up the boat had that sound and motion of when the wind is up. We were doing three knots, then four, five and at times six. So, the last twenty four hours we covered one hundred and nineteen miles. Our best so far is one hundred and thirty eight miles in one day. I don't want it to blow any harder now. Just keep it comfortable and moving.

Our worst day was fifty eight miles. The wind really pooped out and we decided to use the engine. Well, after a few minutes it choked up and stopped. Barry went below to check the fuel lines, etc but all appeared to be in order so we cranked it up again. It started right up but as soon as we put it in gear it stopped. We discovered the problem was one of the lines to a sail was over the side and it had gotten caught up in the propeller. We tried all sorts of things to get it free but nothing worked. The only solution was for Barry to dive on it and cut it free. It was eleven at night when all this happened and I didn't like the idea of him going into the water when it was dark. I could really tell he wanted to go in right at the moment but I got him to wait. We put out the anchor light and went below to get some sleep. Well, a sail boat is much noisier when it isn't sailing and the motion is rolly and neither of us could sleep. Barry was thinking the wind would probably be up in the morning in which case the swells would be too, and then diving would be a lot harder. So, at one in the morning Barry put on his mask and fins, tied a rope around his waist and went over the side. I held on to the other end of the rope in one hand and a flashlight in the other and watched and waited. It didn't take long, just about four dives on it and he cut it free. It was really tangled, the Dacron line melted from the heat of the turning shaft, but his knife was sharp and it was about five minutes at the most he was in the water. I was sure relieved to have him back onboard again. A cup of tea and we both fell asleep letting *Seminole* be hove-to till morning. From now on we will always check to be sure the lines are all safe on deck.

Luckily we have extra line onboard to replace what was damaged.

We spent so much money in Acapulco that towards the end we were getting tired of shopping and short on money. As a result, we are out of vermouth for our sometimes afternoon cocktail. Didn't have much beer to start with which is long gone by now, and with the wine gone too, so much for happy hour. We did buy dried hibiscus flowers in Mexico, and a few buds in a glass of water turn it into a deep pink refreshing drink. Sometimes I wish it were wine. I under-estimated our consumption in a lot of things. Next time I'll have a much better idea of what to take. It is one thousand and fifty miles to the nearest store. Ten more days at four miles per hour. I think sometimes it is sort of crazy to spend one month sailing somewhere I could fly to in five hours. But my house will be there and providing we can find a place to keep the boat in the offseason and there is money to make, we can stay there as long as we want. Anxious to feel the sand under my feet.

We pass the day playing gin rummy, sleeping, reading, eating and thinking. Sort of reminds me of being at Aunt Patty's cabin in Felton on a raining day. It is grey and cloudy outside and not very warm, so we are inside most of the time. It is like you want to go somewhere but not having a car, neighbors, it's Sunday so every place is closed so there is no place to go. No wonder sailors drink ... and we are out of booze.

May 6

It is under six hundred miles now. Hoping to see Maui Sunday afternoon off our port bow. We will be one hundred miles away but it is a tall volcano and should be able to be seen from that distance. It was warm today, laid out in the sun. Spiced beans and chapattis (whole wheat tortillas) for dinner.

May 9

Happy Mother's Day afternoon. We are close enough to Hawaii now we can pick up several radio stations, and of course there are lots of requests. There is one especially pretty song I have been hearing that was played earlier, a Hawaiian song "Hanalei Bay". One verse goes like this, "When you see Hanalei you will be in heaven by the sea." The tune is beautiful and I know you would like it. I must go there and see for myself. I'm really happy out here. It is warm and sunny. We put a blanket over the cockpit for shade.

The sky is blue and the water a deeper blue and up above us are white puffy clouds. Not a whole lot of wind though. Our average has dropped down the last twenty four hours, seventy five miles in all. In fact the last three days have been under one hundred miles a day. But it doesn't matter 'cause it is so fine. This is why we built a boat. Trade wind sailing, want it to last now, no hurry to rush to get there, it will all be over then. Full moon on the thirteenth, and even now on the ninth it casts a lot of light upon the ocean. Enough to read by. Hope to arrive at the channel entrance between Maui and Molokai in the morning of the eleventh. See, when it is good it is great, when it isn't we complain and talk about farms and new boats knowing all along we are going to keep sailing for a long time. We are now thinking of putting a table in so when in port we don't have to eat with plates in our laps and there would be a place to set things down. I think I will put some carpet down too because painted plywood floors are slippery when wet. We are going to put a toilet in also. Then we will sail to the South Pacific and New Zealand. Maybe you will want to fly over on your anniversary.

May 10

On watch, only one more night is between me and a full night sleep. You get used to only three hours of sleep at a time, but to get all eight hours would sure be nice. We should be seeing Maui in the morning. It will take us all day to approach the island. We don't want to anchor at night so we have reduced the sail to go slow.

May 11

We saw the island this morning under a thick layer of clouds. What a thrill! Exactly one month ago we left Manzanillo. It is even hard for me to believe we have been on our way for so long. It really hasn't been a very eventful trip. Not much sea life to speak of, no storms which is fine by me, just a slow laid back trip. We figured out our speed and the distance to Maui and have decided to "heave to" for ten hours and then start sailing around midnight. This way by sunrise we will be close enough to see things better and arrive at the channel at the best time. We can also take the time to get the boat ready for landfall. We need to get the anchor lashed on deck, get some sleep and eat a good meal.

This is as much as I wrote because the next hours we were sailing it was just so grand I could not stop to write. There were rainbows, and a few rain squalls and lots to do to keep busy. Identifying headlands, and enjoying the most wind we had on our entire trip. We set the anchor about eleven in the morning, finished up last night leftovers and fell asleep for a few hours. We had to come down a bit before we could launch the dinghy over the side and row to shore.

All in all it was a good passage. It was a few days longer than we thought, but *Seminole* sails well, gave us back everything we put into her, and promises a lot more in the future.

Love,

Claudette and Barry

CLAUDETTE'S MEATLESS CHILI

This was a *Seminole* staple. All the ingredients could be easily kept aboard and you could eat this out twenty days at sea. It kept great in the pressure cooker pot so you got to eat it for a long time. It was easy to cook, tasted great, and we would make corn bread or tortillas to serve with it. We ate it a lot in Mexico, where we could add different peppers and spices from the local market, which took little side roads around the beans.

Put 2 cups red kidney beans in large pot, soak them until soft, then cook until it all mushes together.

In separate pan add 2 onions chopped, cumin, chili powder and red pepper

Add 1 chopped apple
Moisten up with broth
Add 1 large can of crushed tomatoes with liquid
Cook a bit more.
Add to pot of beans
Then add:
2 tbls diced jalapeno peppers
1 cup canned pineapple pieces
Add little more liquid if necessary

Cook until it looks like chili.
Serve with corn tortillas, grated Monterey Jack Cheese and cut up mango pieces

Serves 6-8 people

Dear Mom

LIFE ONBOARD IN MAUI

This began life in Hawaii and what a life it was. The little harbor was quiet and half empty, the town fell asleep shortly after dark, and it felt like going back in time (for a place in the USA anyway). We were solidly anchored in about sixty feet of water so clear you could always see how the hook was set from the surface. Days passed like water in the river.

We heard about two yoga teachers working for free in the ruins of the old prison. As a daily focus we began to practice with them on the lawn in front of the library. Lined with palm trees and located on the water by the harbor, it was away from the street, making it a perfect place to do yoga. Rising before dawn, we would bathe in the sea, row ashore, do the series and then rest. This would be followed by a wander around the tidy little town picking mangoes, papayas, citrus, and avocados like gathering Easter eggs. By late morning we would row back 'home' where we gave each other massages, read, tinkered with maintenance, or just did nothing.

Money came from doing sail repairs by hand sewing. I could make twenty or thirty dollars for a couple hours work which would buy fresh vegetables

for a few days. And I was making friends throughout the community who were looking for bigger repairs or new sails. Life would be good here, and there were no rules to make us leave this time.

THIS BEGAN LIFE IN HAWAII. WHAT A LIFE IT WAS.

We sailed a lot. Almost every afternoon was a good time to use the perfect sea breeze. Smooth water and just enough wind made the sailing a total pleasure. We would cruise for three or four hours to find ourselves anchored in White Manele Bay on the island of Lanai, where dolphins circled the boat daily, and we heard only the sounds of surf and the big blow holes working. Or we would go to Molokai East shore and hide inside the reef at Pukoo, windy but flat.

Life settled into a simple rhythm of doing what we wanted each day. We lived naked most of the time while in the anchorage and only put on clothes for guests or to go to town. There were half a dozen other boats out there with clothing optional lifestyles too. The daily charter trip of the glass-bottom boat always managed to cruise by to give the tourists a look at ones like us who didn't care. Yoga, swimming, sailing, fishing, cooking, and eating were all we needed to be ready to fall asleep under the stars in the cockpit. I began to wonder what would come next. What was going to happen when we needed to haul? Where would the money come from?

Then Dave Davies found us and made a proposal for us to build a complete set of sails for his gaff-rigged fifty five foot fishing schooner. He said we could come to Oahu, measure the boat, order materials, and he would find us a work space. I needed some major help to do this one since the sails would all be 10.5 ounce and every part of the work would be heavy. Ken Kaufman agreed to sail over with us, and like turtles, we would have our house available for free.

Never having been to Oahu, we had no idea what to expect. Basically it was the big city for us now. With few places available to anchor and be safe, we chose Keehi Lagoon because Dave's boat was at a dock in the marina there. What a horror show compared to the previous months. We had to anchor directly under the flight path of the Honolulu International Airport and were soon wondering if we had lost our way. The area was a hundred percent industrial, dirty and crowded, and there was no respite. But it was good money and the sooner we got it done, the sooner we could turn around and go back to paradise.

The 'work space' turned out to be a windowless room in an unfinished office complex. The main office floor area was open and empty, perfect for the major layouts we would have to do. The sewing and handwork would be done in the little box with the glowing fluorescent lights. For about three weeks we endured the torture of the daily grind, doing our yoga in the morning in the box, then whatever it took to get those heavy sails finished. 10.5 ounce may not seem like much, but when it's layered, patched, roped, and finished with the hardware that was in scale, every operation was a wrestling match for two people, especially when we couldn't spread out in the little room.

Oahu is a dumpster divers dream. Within a few days we had sussed out all the good ones along our route back to the lagoon, and by the time we got back to the boat yard our back-packs and totes would be full of food and fruit from local trees. Figs from the school yard tree by the bus stop, papayas from volunteer plants growing in odd places, lemons, limes, and best of all, whole flats of expensive imported fruit that was tossed every day for being too ripe to sell. It was perfect for us. Ken and I would arrive in the evening and have peaches, pears, and other treats for all the denizens of the marina, far more than we could eat ourselves. We were urban survivors!

When the sails were completed, the schooner wasn't ready for them so we just put them on their deck, got paid, and did some big city shopping before heading back to Lahaina and sanity. That trip is usually not very comfortable, but this time we were treated to a perfect return voyage in smooth water and light trades. In twenty-four hours we were back at anchor in the crystal clear water, with enough city lessons to last us for a long while.

Fate would have it there was another huge opportunity coming our way. Peter Jones owned the schooner *Lavengro* and had a nice house in town. He offered the use of a decent sized room for me to set up the sewing machine and work... especially to work on his awnings. Soon there were repairs galore and all the work for Peter to fill our purse. This made my work even more legitimate in the charter and yacht community, and soon it became known there was a good sailmaker available. Our shopping got easier and life began to be even more relaxed and comfortable.

The fates were kinder still when Harlow Dougherty, a former customer of our San Diego loft, **Sail Services**, flew in just to find me. He heard we were in Lahaina and tracked us down with his unusual request. His fifty-seven foot Alden yawl, *Jada*, was down in Tahiti and needed all new sails. This was a huge job, at least a month of work. Harlow said he would pay half the labor amount in advance and buy all the materials, if I would bring them down in the *Seminole*.

The money would pay for a haulout, some electrical parts to wire the boat and install batteries, buy more food stores, and provide a survival cushion to get into life in the South Pacific. It seemed quite perfect, and after some discussion with Claudette, I said yes to the proposal. We were going to Tahiti and would have a reception committee to help us when we got there.

With the plan in motion I solicited orders around the harbor for new sails. I would go back to California by air, build the sails at Jotz', do all the buying, and arrange shipment to Hawaii. It was October. The first hint of Kona weather was already being seen and it wouldn't be long before the roadstead was not a friendly place like it is in summer. Friends would help Claudette if need be, and everything would be OK.

While I was in California the work went easily. There was stuff to do twenty-five hours a day and with the goal of the South Pacific in mind, the job was a breeze. I was never happier to be laboring in the loft until midnight. Then the letter came.

It was a 'Dear Barry' from Claudette. Full of love but also full of determination to separate our lives and move on. Could I have been so blind to think we were happy? She went to an astrologer in Lahaina and the woman basically told her our stars were now in total conflict and she had to go away from me to fulfill her cosmic plan. Plain and simple she was leaving.

The letter was loving and kind and totally non-threatening. All she wanted was a little house with a picket fence, a garden, and animals. In fact, she said, the life we were living so comfortably and peacefully was not for her, and she would leave as soon as possible. Almost ten years... poof. It had been like a long ride hitchhiking. Now it was time for a new road.

I had no answer. Managing to connect with her by phone, I asked her to get the boat inside the harbor with the help of friends. I would see her when the work was done in a few days and I'd be able to bring the goods home with me. She agreed, the work was done, and the rest was easy.

I arrived back in Maui and within days she was gone. There was no option for us. She asked for nothing. I gave her all the cash I had. She took the two little bags she had when we snuck her away from her parent's house back in '67, literally climbing out the back door window. She was back on the road again. I got a letter some weeks afterwards, and she told me she shaved her legs and armpits, bought some bras, got a driver's license, and started going to discos. I never knew.

It was a blow. The rampant rootlessness just got a strange bump. Suddenly I was alone and responsible for everything, including a large yacht lying at anchor in the open roadstead that left me little time to think about much except following through on the commitments I had obligated myself to financially. Single handing was not my dream, and the sooner I could finish the work ashore, I could begin to think about what it was going to take to get hauled, sail several thousand miles, and build a set of sails in a strange place.

November 25, 1976
Lahaina, Maui

Dear Mom,

A note on Thanksgiving Day to let you know what I have to be thankful for. First off, I'm happy I'm safe inside the harbor. Yesterday and last night it blew pretty hard with big swells and made the anchorage nearly untenable. At around 10am yesterday it was cleared for us to come inside. I got a woman from another boat to give me the little help I needed to get in safely. I could almost have done it alone but it sure is nice to have a hand.

I have my good health, although it's harder to find the time to do yoga and still keep the boat together and work. I'm going to go to Manele Bay and work on the boat when all my debts are paid off and my materials arrive.

I have friends to share the days with but still spend most times in the anchorage alone. Who wants to sit out there?

Life is going much more slowly, taking each day for what it brings rather than for what I want out of it. I could be working long hours but prefer to take things more reasonably. Without a partner who is always there, the work becomes like a prison keeping me alone. I like what I'm doing enough though, so when I'm working its still ok. It's just if I work all the time, I'll never see anything new either (which is some of the reason Claudette left).

She is gone. Psychically gone for sure. No more good feelings. She kind of shut that off for a while as a defense against me. We still talk a lot, but I know it just will never happen again in the same way. She wants a new life with new people and new experiences on her own terms. Her sexuality and love of social and nightlife have been buried too long in our lack of real communication. In short, even though I might change, it's simply too late. I can only wish her the best and treat her with kindness, generosity, consideration, tenderness, and love, whenever I have the chance. I'll do what I can to help her, but my level of responsibility is now so much greater than hers, I feel I can only do so much.

Thanks for sending the money. I'm still going to try to get a new Avon
but other things come first. I think I'll get an outboard and outboard bracket
so I don't have to row as well as do yoga and work. It'll make
life in the anchorage easier.

Say hello to the folks in Sacramento. Let them know sadness soon gives
way to joy as life goes on. Change is healthy for us all and is necessary for
growth. Life's too short for worry and pain. I'll probably write Dad, but in
case I don't get around to it for a while, let him know I'm OK and looking
for a new shipmate.

Love,

Barry

December 20, 1976
Lahaina, Maui

Dear Mom,

Just a note to follow up on our phone conversation. I'm sitting in the cockpit, tied up safely again in the harbor, waiting for the sun to come up. I'm not going to do yoga this morning, just feeling too wiped out from this stupid cold. And today, I've got a load of work to do to keep my obligation to Peter Jones happening. I owe him some covers and cover repairs and need to finish his awnings. When those jobs are done, I'm going to get lots of small boxes and pack and label all my stuff and have it ready to load aboard. That way, when I get the word to move out of the harbor, I can just pack up and go to Lanai for a while.

As far as crew to the South Pacific goes, I'm going to let it take care of itself. I can't walk down the street without being approached by several people, most of them young beautiful women. I'm looking for a competent man, and one or two others. I would like to sail with three, but I would go with four (me and three others).

I have a million things to do today, so I'll cut it off for now. My cold is driving me nuts, but for the first time I'm ignoring it and making out fine. There's no one here to give me any pity so I just do what I have to do.

Please have no tears or sad thoughts; I am doing exactly what I want to be doing and most happy doing it. You having a good Christmas will make me the happiest. I'll be with you in my thoughts.

Love,

Barry

The *Seminole* and I did a lot of wonderful day sailing with the folks in the yoga group, and there were always plenty of people to spend a warm afternoon gliding along the shores of West Maui. The 'loft' at Jones' was broken down bit by bit and moved back aboard. The stern cabin and two other lockers were crammed full of bolts of cloth, tapes, hardware, rope, and small tools. The stored food we had put aboard in San Diego was still in fine shape, so I could live for almost nothing. With no beer, wine, tobacco, cheese, and bread in our diet, the food budget was tiny and the haulout budget was ready.

When Claudette left the island I was beat down, torn up, and wondering what would be the next move. However, Lahaina was a destination for wanderers and experimental living and it wasn't long before things got sort of crazy.

It wasn't as bad as I thought. Linda was looking for a ride to Tahiti on the bulletin board at the Harbormaster's office. A lovely blonde traveler, backpack living.

"Sure", I said. "How about going to Lanai for a few days? You chip in on food and we are there."

So we trooped down the street to go to the market, and ran into Kite Store Nancy, about the same age as Linda and always a ton of laughs. When she heard we were going to Lanai, she said she'd chip in too. At the market, Jenny, a woman more my age who was always friendly, saw us and within ten minutes of conversation she was going too. We loaded with groceries and just like that, were sailing away. Before we were two miles out they had all stripped naked and all I could do was try and keep it real.

We had such a great time surfing, diving, and just hanging out. Linda made the move and that led to us having some time together after getting back from Lanai. Then about a week later she told me she had a ride south on another boat that was leaving the next day. Oh well. Back to basics again.

Maybe having a nice yacht anchored in paradise is attractive (regardless of your empty pockets) because the next month was punctuated by a series of brief encounters with interesting ladies, and one dose of the crabs that created lots of trips to shore washing bedding and trying to drive the little buggers from my home. The Silversword lady gave me the gift that keeps on giving.

After my bout with parasites I slowed down considerably and concentrated on getting my butt in gear, finishing the details of many small jobs. And I felt much more rational after having to deal with all the consequences of profligate living. But fate had other things in mind.

One afternoon I went to Jones' and he came to the door looking pretty wrecked. We chatted some and shared some herb and he told me he found my crew for Tahiti. He said this woman was French and very exciting. The way he looked, the fact it was about three in the afternoon and he was just getting into the light, said lots. Intriguing.

From the hallway we heard, "Cheri??"

Then she was there. The woman on the silver bicycle in the leopard skin bikini, the one with the copper hair, green eyes, ivory armband, and the huge chunk of amber dangling along with a small leather juju sack around her neck... I had seen her many times and always watched in wonder. Her khaki safari thing was well unbuttoned still, and the skirt, short but a little crooked. Jones had been conservative.

He spoke decent French and acted as the translator. He sold the whole deal. When she asked if I was going to sail to Tahiti, I easily said, "Would you like to go?"

With no hesitation she said, "OK... we go!" Just like that.

The *Seminole* was in a slip in Manele Harbor. Another boat had ferried me to Lahaina and the *Searunner* schooner was my ride back to Manele. We had about an hour to get aboard. We separated, agreeing to meet in the harbor and I thought, no way was she going to show up. She did.

Thereupon I entered another realm of consciousness, a place I never imagined, challenges I would have never created for myself, all now destined to play out as life with Amber Shock. But that's another story.

Then she was there.

The woman on the silver bicycle
in the leopard skin bikini,
the one with the copper hair, green eyes,
ivory armband, and the huge chunk of amber dangling
along with a small leather juju sack around her neck.

I entered another realm
of consciousness.

Dear Mom,

I'm taking the time now before things get too crazy to let you in on the hot poop. Tomorrow midnight, *Seminole* and crew goes to Oahu for preparation to make the passage to Tahiti. We'll be there for about three weeks, working hopefully. Then back to Lahaina for as little time as possible. Perhaps one week. Then to Kealakekua (Big Island) to take fresh stores and rest a few days. Hopefully, we'll be underway by February 7-15th.

The passage should be approximately twenty to thirty days, arriving in Papeete by mid-March. Allowing two weeks settling time and two months work time, I could be ready for new adventures by mid-May.

Honolulu will also be visa and consulate time. The woman who may sail with me is thirty-three, a French citizen, speaks French, Spanish, Portuguese, two African dialects, English, and has traveled a great deal. She's an absolute monster. Unique. Free. She's physically powerful, able to free dive to fifty-sixty feet and swim outrageously. Just going for it all the time. Spontaneous and no bullshit. And, unbelievably beautiful. Striking carved features, superb figure, hair like flame, and skin golden or caramel. I'm almost afraid to believe it's real. Like some dream she came along and tore me away from everything I thought, and showed me a space where there is no time, no hurry, only two in the universe. Exotic and ever-changing.

I know I could never possess her even for a moment. It would be like trying to hold the wind or the sunlight. But nonetheless, I burst with the anticipation of sharing some time together. Her name is Amber Schock. It's not too often you meet someone who can take tomorrow away.

The other person is a twenty-four year old man named Tim. He's been mate on a sixty foot schooner around here for a year or so. Neither Amber nor Tim has experience with crossing oceans, but neither did I. Have to start somewhere.

I certainly didn't mean for you to spend so much. The prices I was told were in the $350-$400 range. Perhaps the New Year brought us new prices. I'll send you some extra to help cover. I need the dinghy worse than money. Tomorrow we're going to do Robert's oarlocks. This is something that is greatly appreciated. He knows you fronted the bread and it's coming in this letter.

I still have no sense of how to tell the folks what's going on. How do I say the scene is different? Or should I bother. My last letter sort of made it obvious I was alone in this venture now. If they ask – don't bullshit them. Just tell them straight. If they don't ask...don't say anything.

January 15, 1977

Sorry for the delay but I had to battle a very serious bacterial infection which made my elbow swell to double size and gave me a very high temperature. Had to resort to the emergency room in the hospital. It's been hard on me all round, especially the morale.

I'm going to try and get an old pair of prescription sunglasses put together. They'll need one new lens at least. You've done too much already. I'll take care of it somehow.

Love,

Barry

BARRY'S SHRIMP EXTRAORDINAIRE

One whole sweet onion
1 tsp Curry paste
1 tsp brown sugar
Bamboo shoots
1/3 cup clam juice
2/3 cup vegetable broth
1/3 cup peas from the pod
2/3 cup coconut cream
1 1⁄2 lb shelled medium shrimps

1 onion, cut up and cook in vegetable oil, stirring few minutes
Add 1 rounded tsp green curry sauce
And 1 heaping tsp brown sugar

Add can of bamboo shoots, cut up
Add clam juice and vegetable stock

1⁄2 cup of peas from pod – cook quickly then blanch in ice water
Add 2/3 cup coconut cream
Add shelled medium shrimps

Keep cooking until pink.

Add basil toward end – serve over rice

Serves 4 to 5 people

February 28, 1977
Lahaina, Maui

Dear Mom,

I'm using this quiet day as an opportunity to convey to you some of my thoughts before leaving on this passage to the South Pacific. It seems strange now to be sitting in my cockpit hearing the voices of three new people, especially when the language is French. All of the crew are now French people. Tim, the only American onboard left in Lahaina because he couldn't handle my wild French lady. She seemed a most unlikely boat lady, but has become a real part of the crew, cooking when others can't even be below, and learning "the ropes" like any good sailor should. It will take a bit longer because of the language difference, but with the others speaking French and having good experience, we all learn fast.

Jerome is going to Tahiti to serve his French military duty. He's twenty-one years old and madly in love with the daughter of famous American circumnavigator, William Albert Robinson, who now lives in Tahiti. He's a fine young man, willing, and with some experience. Can't cook though. We now have a "key" when we get to Tahiti as we have a 'package' to deliver to Robinson's oldest daughter, and permission to use a mooring which was for his boat, a seventy-three foot brigantine, the *Varua*, now in service with a whale conservation group.

Patrick is thirty-four and so similar in experiences and chronology to me, it's strange. We even share the same birthday! He built a forty-two foot Block Islander in ferro-cement and sailed it for almost seven years before losing it on a reef in the Tuamotus. He then lived on Ahe' Atoll for two years, where he built an island style house, did lobster farming and fishing, and still has many friends among the islands sixty inhabitants. This will be our first stop, a place I'm sure will be hard to leave.

Patrick has access to arable land with plenty of fresh water on Tahiti-iti, very close to where Harlow and the *Jada* are. We intend to help each other build shelter and workspace and I'll set up my stuff out in the boonies, if possible. I'm putting a lot of faith in him right now to be able to help me stay in Tahiti for a while. I'm also very excited about having a land place again. Patrick and I have similar thoughts about boats and life, and we both seem to seek the same things.

Amber is thirty-four with hair like flames, green eyes, and skin of bronze. She's a mystical woman, full of potions and lotions and little secret things. We fight and love like the best of friends and have overcome a good many differences of opinion and lifestyle already. I don't put our lives together beyond today, and really could wish for no more. A day with her smile and beauty and energy are more than enough for this one man. It has been a very tough time for her as she has been used to complete individual freedom for as long as I've been married. And now she has to deal with living in a very small space on the boat with the same people for long periods of time.

Seminole is as ready as she will ever be to sail south. Maintenance wise she is suffering and needs tender care badly. Topsides, decks, cabins, spars, all need work. But she still sails good even though loaded down with all my sail loft materials to build all the sails for a sixty foot yawl and more, gear for three crew members, extra food stores for living ashore, etc, etc.

These last days have been spent at Kealakekua Bay near Captain Cook on the big island of Hawaii. It's a quiet, peaceful place with fruit and vegetables in abundance. Very volcanic and dry near the sea, with more green as you go higher.

Last night we stayed at a friend's place about a mile from here. Called "The Pavilion" by him, and rightly so because of its size. It's a huge building, perhaps two hundred feet square, all open to the forest in back and the sea in front. Palms and papayas all round. A very Zen place, all this space with almost nothing in it, except a table, a few chairs and several beds. Oh, and a fine wood fire sauna which we all enjoyed, followed by a dive into the moonlit sea. At night it rained buckets on the tin roof of this place. The sound was incredible.

This morning we are doing a last laundry and getting vegetables and more oranges, bananas and papayas. I'm writing this now in the P.O.

Lately, I've been thinking much of this trip to Tahiti and hope to have a space where I could call home base for a while and leave my tools and "sail loft". A garden and a little house with a hammock and a kitchen of sorts would be nice. I'm hoping you can come to stay with me in a place like this for a while. Perhaps a three-week period would convince you to retire and live in a quiet green place.

This letter has taken several days to write because of the hustle of last minute things. If you would share it with the folks and Dad, I'd appreciate it. It's so difficult to communicate during these times of being here and there and at sea. I've been in ten different places in the last eighteen days and spent five or six days as sea just moving around the Hawaiian Islands. You can write c/o Yacht *Seminole*, Poste Restante, Taravao, Tahiti, French Polynesia from now on. I won't be there until probably April 15th, so don't expect any reply much before 1st of May.

Love you all from me and Amber and Patrick and Jerome.

Barry

*Water would be precious considering we had to allow
for being three more weeks at sea,
at a gallon a day for all of us.*

MAUI TO TAHITI

**March 1977 to April 1977
Maui to Tahiti**

After filling every space below with fresh food, including coconuts, oranges, papayas, grapefruits, bananas, cabbage, and onions, we made the decks ready for the ocean passage. All the loose junk was secured or put below, and the bottom scrubbed. We were smooth, clean, and ready to go.

The crew consisted of Patrick Humbert, Jerome from France, and Amber Shock. With two of the crew having no experience sailing, let alone crossing oceans, this was set to be an interesting voyage at the least.

The first week we pounded every mile to weather because the wind was below East, making it hard to get far enough over to make our destination. Those days were draining and challenging in so many ways. The constant heeling, pitching into the giant trade wind swells, spray and water everywhere, made us crave some shift in the wind, something to make it easier.

Several days out, Amber had some cooking going down below. While sitting on the cabin sole lodged in a corner, she was making pancake dough. When ready to cook the flapjacks, she started making her way around the cabin carrying something in each hand when there was a particularly wild lurch over a big swell. She flew across the cabin and smacked the back of her head hard against the mast. She lay bleeding and moaning for a few minutes before anyone realized she was in trouble.

The three of us helped her into the cockpit, since down below was a mess of pancake dough and blood all over the sole. Amber was groggy and relatively calm. I got out the first aid kit while Patrick washed the wound. It was a big cut messed up with hair, so we went for the scissors and razor. A few quick snips and some swipes with a razor and we had a clean area around the wound. A good wash with mild soap and some pressure on the wound made the bleeding slow enough so we could apply butterfly strips and cover the whole thing with gauze. Then we did a head wrap under her chin and around the forehead for the final touch.

While I was cleaning up the bloody mess below, Amber became aware and really angry we had cut her beautiful hair. Soon the three of them were in a raging argument in French so I decided to stay below and out of the way. Patrick took the blame for the wound fix and gave every bit of it back to her when she complained. This totally set the stage for the rest of the trip. Nothing about this passage was going to be normal.

The days passed with the weather turning more northeast as we made our way south and a bit east. This made the sailing gentler and put less strain on the crew. The next emergency came soon though when I found water in my navigation area lockers and the books were all wet. Where had this come from?

It turned out when Patrick was opening the deck fittings for the water tanks he used a small center punch instead of the normal wrench made for the job. This punched a tiny hole in the cap. The fitting was almost constantly underwater when the rail was down while we were going to weather hard. The motion of the boat sloshed the water in the tanks, creating a vacuum suction that pulled seawater in through the tiny hole. The tanks were interconnected by a valve system which allowed them to be drained one at a time. Sadly, two of them were open to each other and the sea filled them enough to overflow from the vents that went up under the deck level, and poor me thinking there would never be an overflow for any reason.

We had two tanks totally fouled with salt water, and the third was OK. Now about ten days out, we were already down to about thirty-five gallons of good water, plus our six gallon emergency stash. From then on there would be little use of fresh water for anything but cooking and drinking. Water would be precious considering we had to allow for being three more weeks at sea. At a gallon a day for all of us, that final tank would be just enough.

After all that excitement, the days seemed to blend together in the routine of watch keeping and daytime activities of cooking, cleaning, and minding the ship. The wind direction backed so we could ease sheets, and each day it got lighter and more comfortable. There were weird happenings between the crew members, especially Amber and I, and the dynamic of the interaction makes a complete story on its own. Another story.

Light winds made life aboard most comfortable. By this time, we were all living naked, and had worked out the watch schedules that fit us together best. There was a batik dyed sheet over the center cockpit behind the spray dodger. This turned the middle of the boat into a kind of nomad's heaven with soft cushions and pillows, incense, playing cards, and books for reading in the shady comfort. The boat would steer herself with the wind vane for hours without touching anything. Music drifted from the stereo. We floated on the ocean.

On the day we were supposed to cross the equator, the sea was inviting. The sky was almost cloudless, only the darkest blue below. Our morning sun sight was already showing almost ninety degrees and we would be there most of the day. The heat fit with the searing sun directly overhead almost all day long. We had no ice or booze, so it was popcorn and Big Island oranges for our banquet. We hung out in the patterned light doing our best to stay on deck and in the coolest place.

WE WERE ABOUT AS FAR AS YOU CAN GET FROM ANY LAND ON THE PLANET. IT WAS AROUND TWELVE HUNDRED MILES TO HAWAII, A BIT LESS TO TAHITI, AND THOUSAND MORE IN THE OTHER DIRECTIONS.

By noon we were almost perfectly on the Equator. Because we had imagined it so much, the ocean and the sky conspired to have us experience a true noon day sun, and it was a hang dog day in the heat. The wind was around three to five knots, barely rippling the surface, perfect for the full main, drifter, and light weight stays'l. With a low, long, ground swell we were gliding along with pressure in the sails, heeled a few degrees. The quiet was distracting.

Then we heard the gasp of air exhaled and taken, the breath. Whale!

We threw open the sides of the tent, and off our starboard beam was a large whale, perhaps as long as the boat. It had taken a position alongside, about twenty feet or so from our rail. One enormous left eye was looking at us, scanning from bow to stern.

We all got on deck and stood at the lifelines, four naked humans, nothing to say. It watched.

WE WERE IN THE MIDST OF A CETACEAN CONVENTION!

We were about as far as you can get from any land on the planet. It was around twelve hundred miles to Hawaii, a bit less to Tahiti, and thousands more in the other directions.

The chances of another human being within a thousand miles were more than slim. It was definitely a visit.

Then Patrick saw other whales off the bow. Soon there were whales everywhere. He and I went up the mast to the spreaders and saw dolphins leaping and whales spouting as far as could be seen in any direction.

When we got down from the height, Patrick went below and placed the stereo speakers next to the hull. He cued up Paul Horn playing in the Great Pyramids to the track with the whale sounds, and cranked the volume full on. Now the whales really knew we were there.

Even though the boat was only just making way, the big old whale slid along right next to us, looking, always looking with his big eye, an eye as big as a football. Everywhere we looked, we still saw whales and dolphins. Spinners were leaping, and bigger ones wheeling along in large pods. We were in the midst of a cetacean convention!

We must have been attractive out there, with our light weight genoa in bright yellow, a huge orange sunburst appliquéd in the middle. The genoa stays'l was light blue with an Earth sewn in, and a view of the Pacific side of the planet showed. Our tanbark red mainsail rounded out the odd and brilliant color scheme. We discussed what it was that would bring these hundreds, if not thousands of performing beings, out to greet us on this auspicious day. The Equator at Equinox.

After about ten minutes, the big old boy who was watching us made a couple of wheeling moves and slid away. The others had been dwindling. Soon, the sea was empty and we were alone again. The breeze was steady and the *Seminole* hardly moved, doing two or three knots. Dreamy.

But the Universe saved the big one for last with the sunset from heaven. I don't know if something odd happens when you see a sunset at the Equator on the Equinox, but somehow it did to us. As the sky fell into deeper twilight, it appeared there was a golden dividing line of light across the cosmos. Stars were visible, can't remember the moon phase, but this sky was like it was split in two, horizon to horizon. The effect was short-lived, an afterglow, witnessed again in silent awe, simple naked humans treading the boundaries of space on a wet planet.

South of the equator seemed a different world. The soft wind held steady and we aimed directly at our goal, Ahe'. The plan was to spend time where Patrick lived on his little motu, and to visit and help Bernard Moitessier with his garden project. Each day the wind got a little stronger and most of the weirdness had passed into the wake.

Everyone seemed OK except Jerome. He had become very unstable. Other than what he absolutely had to do to stand his watch, he was basically catatonic, lying in his bunk and staring at the overhead. There was fear in his voice and several times he came up the companionway in the middle of our night watch, screaming we were in a storm. In fact, it was perfect conditions and the boat was churning miles in total control. Amber managed to calm him, but after those times he was never the same.

As we closed on Ahe' the importance of our navigation ramped up. The sky was brilliantly clear and evening star sights were a great addition to the normal sun lines we had been using. I managed to get a good three planet fix just two days out and we were right on our target course. Atolls are often only a few meters of elevation above sea level, and the coconut trees are all you might see from six or eight miles off, if you get lucky.

The navigation was good, and around noon of the twenty-third day we were finding our way into the narrow channel leading to the huge lagoon. At that point Patrick had the con from the spreaders and we glided in. Bernard's *Joshua* was clear in the distance and our little engine carried us those last miles before we dropped the anchor a hundred yards from shore. Bernard was already rowing out to greet us.

There were still half a dozen fresh oranges and a pineapple left. To be sitting in our cockpit sharing fruit and talking with my hero was amazing. We laughed and talked like old friends and then followed Bernard ashore to see his little fare' and meet his wife, Illena, and young son, Stephan. They were living on the motu called Poro Poro in a garden setting of simple intensity. The house opened east to west and you could see the sunrise or the sunset from the upper floor 'room'. There was almost no 'furniture' or kitchen, and life was harsh, simple, and focused on the needs of the place. The organic garden needed water and work on the compost, fish traps had to be tended, and there was always work on the house and the water catchment system so Bernard could keep his crop of tomatoes and cucumbers happy.

We had a week of total immersion in atoll life. We dined with the chief and his family, dove and spear fished surrounded by packs of blacktip sharks, and took the *Seminole* to the weather end of the island to carry humus back to Bernard's garden. After the last day spent moving dinghy loads to the boat, our deck was stacked with flour sacks full of this rich black mulch.

One of the island guys asked us to join in the hunt for delicious coconut crabs. An adventure not to be forgotten, we went around the dense forest in the afternoon tying big hunks of coconut flesh to the tree trunks just high enough for the giant crabs to reach them. Then we waited until midnight for the greedy guys to grab on and be ready for the taking. We ran through the black dark forest following this islander, his pressure lamp swinging wildly as he leaped big roots and fallen branches to grab hold of these giant tree crabs with huge claws. It was true adventure, and eating them was a taste treat, coconut flavored delicate meat in a single huge claw.

Jerome was pressing us to get him to Tahiti so he would be on time for his deployment. He had moved off the boat and was living in the structure that had been Patrick's home. I think he had enough of us 'old' weirdoes and couldn't wait to be away from us. When we arrived in Ahe' he got off as soon as possible and stayed away until we told him it was time to go. We had two or three days left to be together and then he would be free of us.

Almost the minute we passed the lines ashore to stern tie to the quay in Papeete, Jerome was ashore with his gear bag. We had to meet him again later for the immigration and clearance, and we got to meet William Albert Robinson and his three beautiful daughters. That was perhaps the last period during which things would be 'normal' in Tahiti. Our plan was to explore the place we would build the sails, heal my infected foot from Ahe', and Patrick was the key to making it all happen. For him it was like being home. For me it was a swirling series of events and uncertainties with plenty of obstacles and resistance just to make it interesting.

Bernard Moitessier's ***Joshua*** *was clear in the distance and our little engine carried us those last miles before we dropped anchor a hundred yards from shore. Bernard was already rowing out to greet us.*

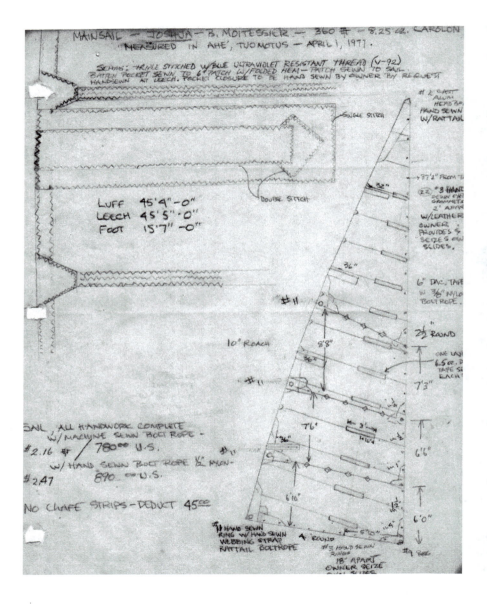

BERNARD MOITESSIER

When our boat building dream was gaining steam, both Claudette and I read every book possible on small boat voyaging. Two characters stood out as having the kind of inspiration I always felt myself. They were William Albert Robinson and Bernard Moitessier.

We followed Bernard's exploits through his amazing books and the news that was available. I had heard from my friends in Tahiti he was there and took the chance to write him at an address someone gave me. My letter was full of questions about heavy weather handling, choosing between a ketch and cutter rig, and general questions about sailing long distance. To my surprise, after three months, I received a wonderful carefully hand written reply. This began a correspondence that continued for years, until just months before we left Hawaii to sail to the Tuamotus.

When we sailed into the lagoon and anchored next to *Joshua,* I felt as though I had completed some sort of pilgrimage. When he got to our boat, we shared gifts from Hawaii and talked like normal folks who already knew quite a bit about each other, from Patrick, and from our correspondence. The fact of actually being there had still not settled in and I found myself staring at the palm lined beach, the crystal water, and *Joshua's* red hull, thinking it was some kind of dream.

Through the years of admiring Bernard's life and his style, I exposed many of my friends to him and his philosophy of the sea. Ken Kaufman and I made shoes from canvas and tires based on a description in one of his books, and proudly wore them as our 'Bernards', as we studied every grainy black and white photo in his books to glean details of what was working almost flawlessly. And the shoes were so cheap.

Bernard was a character who personally did many things to help life on the little island. He brought cats from Tahiti to keep the rat population down. They were destroying the coconut crop. By example, he showed the people the way to create soil and expand their diet. His days were filled with hard, physical work, and his wiry physique showed his fitness. Climbing coconut trees was not a problem. Diving, swimming, walking... he led the pace.

Bernard talked about having some sails made somewhere, so as a favor, we went out to *Joshua* to take measurements for her sails. I had tapes and tools and left him with a full document, along with offsets and hardware specifications. The real treat was getting to explore the boat. To experience this craft that had taken him safely around the world several times, mostly alone, was truly enlightening. I built a yacht, he built a sailing boat.

Welds weren't ground. There was nothing but paint. The masts, made from telephone poles, still oozed creosote in the heat. Cable clamps and chain were used in places I wouldn't have expected. As in the photos from '**The Long Way**', the same truck tire inner tube was on the foredeck vent. *Joshua* had nothing unnecessary and it all worked perfectly. And she had always been enough for Bernard, because it was being at sea that counted, and this boat had little else.

Down below was even more the lesson. All the ribs were exposed, hard edges and corners ready to attack your head or body. There was no 'liner', no softness, just a simple bunk and a table to work on, and lots of big canvas bags, sails, and rope hanging against the inner hull. The two by twelve board seat hung from chains, the wash basin turret still there ready to go back to the Southern Ocean again. It was all painted white, clean and simple, just perfect. As he said, there was no time for fancy stuff when there was sailing to be done.

After meeting in Ahe', I only saw Bernard in Tahiti a few more times. Somehow Patrick knew when he was in town and we would meet up for some beers and a good yarn. We sailed away to end up in New Zealand, spent seven months away only to meet up again on Mo'orea, where he had *Joshua* anchored while living ashore in a small house on the hillside. His wife, Ileana, was making artistic pareus with solar dyes and native plant designs. They had no more in this home than on motu Poro Poro. Simple always did fine. Happiness was everywhere.

Later in Maui we made a new main for *Joshua*, and Bernard was able to use it enough to give feedback before he lost *Joshua* in Cabo San Lucas. He sailed again on the *Tamata*, and I heard tales of his travels from others. Then he was gone, a victim of all those Gauloise he smoked all day long. His legacy of words will live on long after him and serve to inspire many others to take up time on the sea.

We can all be grateful there are such humans to give us pause to think about the alternatives to what is 'normal'.

Dear Barry

Joshua arrived 10 days ago
in San Francisco, from Tahiti,
(good trip, 38 days, no hurricane,
lots of light winds, but fair, also
some force 5-6.)

I wanted to tell you that
the main you made fits very
well, good performances I think.
thanks.

I expect to stay for a long
while in the states. Hélène and
Stephan will follow later, by plane
(I came alone). I droped anchor
in Sansalito, nice peoples. I
will try to make some lectures
with a 40 minutes color film
that I made during the long
voyage 12 years ago.

Love
Bernard

He who loses his hat

to the wind

Has not tied the string

at his chin.

Finding all the lovable capable beautiful parts.

Be honest.

Although you may want to share with her, she has moved on.

Grow with her.

Move on.

It has changed with the Dragon Fly's Eyes.

Caught in my sight

What a light in the

Dragon Fly's eyes.

Like windows of fire

Into the changing moment.

Taking the next curve

Was somehow

Different.

Floating into release

And up again.

Smiling

Breathing easy.

GO WITH WHAT YOU GOT

More down than up
Sucks the wind.
She was always so sad
To be with me
And could never see
How far away she stayed
Oh well.

The moonlight on Haleakala
And the Dragon Fly's eyes
Were enough for this evening.
You're going to have a great deal
Of nervous energy to deal with this weekend.
Oh well.

Goodbye – none.
Don't care no more.
She can piss up a rope
There now that feels better.

It will be a pleasure,
Whatever was in the Dragon Fly's eyes.
Changes for sure.

You can't find out where the middle is
unless you've been at both ends.

Dear Mom TAHITI

JAMAICAN PORK TENDERLOIN

My cousin, Greg Clausen, is a Master Chef, educated at the California Culinary Institute, a top chef in major restaurants, and is currently a private chef to a large corporation.

He invited me to his house for a cook together. I read this thing in an airplane magazine about Jamaica flavors and the way they cooked pork tenderloin, so decided to try it out with he and his family.

Mix 1/4 parts of cayenne pepper, nutmeg, allspice, garlic salt.
Cut tenderloin into 1/2 inch slices.
Pound between wax paper and dip in spices.
Fry in butter & oil.

Serve with Vegetables – red, yellow, green pepper strips, green onions cut on diagonal with chili peppers.

Yummy!

Dear Mom,

Please see everyone knows we've arrived safe and satisfied. I've been having my own problems here and have neglected communication. We arrived a week ago and have been dealing with the immediate problems of how to keep it together and get it together here, money and work wise.

This next month or so will tell a lot about whether or not I'll stay. Making plans now is extremely difficult, but it's in my mind to get back to San Francisco to work with Roger around mid-July if possible. Perhaps I'll sail, I don't know. I'll know more when Harlow's sails are done.

I'm not going to elaborate on anything right now because of the confusion here. The voyage was the finest ever. Our stay in the Tuamotus superb. I have a long letter to Claude, which may never get mailed because things are changing so rapidly.

I'm glad for your trip to Spain as you would've found me doing nothing much but working here. So have a ball and don't worry about me. I'm thirty years old now and have finally reached the point where I'm alone enough to work things out for myself.

Sorry for the brevity but it's necessary now as there is so little time before you leave to let you know I'm OK. I have a friend in Patrick, and everyday simply gets better. Give my love to Claude please.

All my love,

Barry

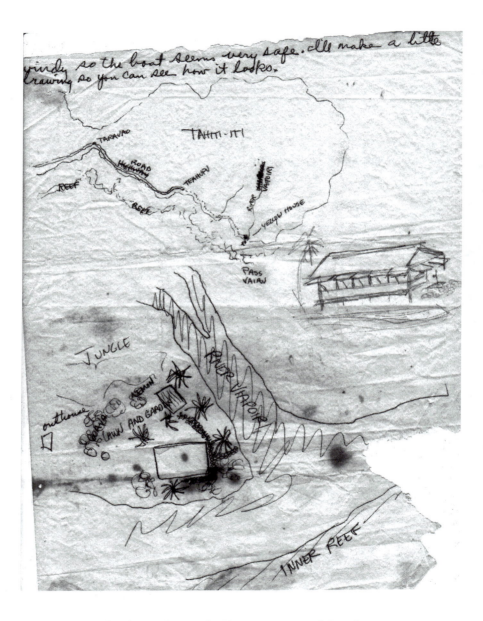

*I feel as though I've come a bit closer
to having paradise within me as well.*

May 15, 1977
Teahupo, Tahiti

Dear Mom,

This fine Sunday morning finds me in the best of spirits. Many things have changed since the last letter I wrote. Our scene here is now fairly comfortable and together. My first letter was written in haste to guarantee you'd have word from me before you left for Spain. I had a bad infection on my foot and was battling with Amber. There was obstacle after obstacle in getting work here. Things have now evolved into a very gentle space. Amber has been back with me for a month or so, with much happiness. Although she is now leaving again, there are less hard feelings this time.

Patrick and I work well together and we have a fine place for the boat and the "loft". Papeete is just like any other big city; cars and concrete, dirty and uptight. Getting away from there did the trick. We couldn't leave until about ten days ago because immigration and port officials refused to let us go. None of us had any money for the security bond, so we conned them with the cruiser's cooperative bond fund. (When it is time to bond your crew, you gather money from all the sailors, show it, then gave it all back.) The same money bonded more than one boat for sure. And now I'm in paradise.

THE WATER INSIDE THE REEF RANGES FROM SIXTY TO A HUNDRED FEET DEEP AND IS CRYSTAL CLEAR.

Paradise is a little yellow house on the southwest end of Tahiti in the Teahupo district. The closest "civilization" is the town of Taravao (one store, a pharmacy, and a post office). It is about fifteen km away; seven or eight km either by dinghy or a fairly rugged footpath, the rest by bus or hitchhike. There are perhaps twenty families along this seven or eight km walk, most of them Tahitian, living very simply. All the shoreline is protected by a large reef about half km off shore. The water inside the reef ranges from sixty to a hundred feet deep and is crystal clear. Because of the reef, the anchorage is very flat even when it's windy, so the boat seems very safe. I'll make a little drawing so you can see how it looks.

BARRY SPANIER

The house sits on a point of land at the mouth of a river twenty to thirty meters wide and two meters deep. The river is sort of "plugged" by the inner reef and is fresh water on top with salt water twelve inches below the surface and goes up about a half km into the jungle. There it's flowing faster, tumbling over rocks green with moss, a color like I've never seen before.

Soft green color

In the rushing waters

The mountain flows to the sea.

The house has a wood floor and walls about two feet high. It is open completely on all sides with big panels of plywood hinged on the top so we can close it up if necessary. The sea... that is the lagoon... laps gently on the shore, about ten meters from the house. Seven good-sized trees grow along the water's edge.

We've taken out a wall, painted the floor bright yellow, and now have a clean, fairly large place to work. There is a 'storeroom' and a kitchen but no running water. For water, we merely walk up this beautiful river to where the water is all clean and fresh, and fill a jerry can. Usually I bathe and wash some clothes on a big smooth stone, then with the laundry and water jugs floating in a big tub, swim downstream to the sea and the house.

We also hauled hundreds of large flat stones from farther up the stream to build a walkway around the house, keeping the dirt down. Soon, we'll have a path to the garden and outhouse, but it is going to require some time.

The coconut trees in the yard provide drinking nuts and nutmeat anytime we want it. The guavas are out of season now. There are oranges and avocadoes up the valley and shrimps in the river. Taro and yams can also be found, if you hunt around. The garden is still pretty much a goal rather than a reality, but will give us tomatoes, spinach, okra, cabbage, onions, parsley, radishes and beans.

I've been doing yoga every morning, swimming, and working hard all day.

We eat well and I feel healthy and strong with no more infection. Work on the sails started a week ago and they are all cut except the largest and soon I'll be sewing. Needless to say it's pretty nice working with the trees, birds, sea, and sky all round.

Getting to this point has taken much longer than anticipated and I am no longer putting any pressure on myself to get things done in a hurry. I still want to get back to the city, but how or when is going to be left to the fates. Right now, I haven't enough money to provision the boat or fly, but perhaps if I can work for Roger, it will happen. In the meanwhile, I'm going to live and work here in peace and quiet; grow things, walk in the forest, and swim in the sea. The view from the boat at anchor is worth the swim out there. All incredibly green, with soft white clouds laying in the valleys, waterfalls, and my little yellow house by the river (rent free too!).

And each day I feel as though I've come a bit closer to having paradise within me as well. Calming my mind and quiet my spirit, so the anger that so often makes me sad has no place in my life. I think I can go back to the city now and see it merely as part of the whole, and accept it as necessary phase of human evolution.

So Ma, I'm happy and together. I'd like you to share this with everyone who would care. As I have adventures, I'll continue to relate them. Next time, I might even have a photo if I'm lucky. Give my love to Dad and Veronica especially. He'd be happy to know I can sit in my home/loft looking at *Seminole* anchored in the lagoon so quiet, hearing the sound of the sea so near. The only part I couldn't keep together was my life with Claude, but perhaps she'll see this place someday too. Meanwhile everything is just as it should be, no more, no less, all by the grace of God. Maruru Teatua.

I'orana and love,

Barry

PS Every afternoon when the land breeze comes up, beautiful red and yellow flowers float down the river to the sea, blown from the trees up the valley by the wind.

BARRY SPANIER

Dear Mom,

Saturday afternoon and the sun is setting again on another one of those days in paradise. I'm sitting here looking out on my little world, listening to the birds and watching the afternoon's activities. The land crabs are cleaning up the yard, picking up anything loose on the ground and scurrying back into their holes. The local insect orchestra is tuning up for another evening serenade, and the surf is breaking especially heavy on the outer reef. Must be fifteen-foot waves thundering down full force on the coral. Very loud even from half a mile away. The colors this time of day are very accentuated, especially the golden burau flowers (the ones that float down the river) along with the brilliant red hibiscus blossoms. These trees surround the house so when the wind blows hard, we have to sweep the flowers off the floor inside.

The last two days have been clear and sunny with puffy trade wind clouds and grand sunsets. Today was the third day of a five-day holiday on the island so we've had many folks tramping through, just sightseeing. Nobody we knew. We haven't had any visitors yet, though it would be nice. Patrick and I seem to be good company for each other and have enough to talk about to keep it interesting. Amber has gone away, probably for good this time. Although who knows. I really cared for her but we just can't live together. She wasn't happy unless we were playing all the time.

The real part of my being here, the sails, is allowing little time for that now, as I've decided to return to S.F. It is important for me to clear up this whole thing with Claude and get on to something else. Beside, *Seminole* needs to do more sailing before we part. She looks so fine right now; her hull is golden in the last light, complimented by a bunch of pink clouds in a pale blue sky.

In many ways, I'd like to stay right here for a while, but one more time, the timing is off. If we wait much longer than July, it gets chancy for hurricanes just north of the Equator, the ones that come off the Central American coast. As it is, we'll have to be listening to the weather very closely.

This place has such potential. With several months of work on the house and garden one could be almost self-sufficient, requiring visits to town only when you want to go, instead of having to go for fresh food. We do quite well around here with fruit, but we still have to go to Teahupo to scrounge. If we could live here for long term, there could be bananas, papaya, pomplemous (a huge sweet grapefruit growing everywhere, just for the picking). Plus there are avocado, mango and orange trees nearby. A vegetable garden would take at least two months and a lot of energy to produce anything. Perhaps I'll return, and then you'll be able to ride across the lagoon and experience the breathtaking beauty.

If you're going to be gone for the month of June, I won't write again until around mid-June. I'll write Dad and Veronica and the old folks though, and you'll have something in your mailbox when you return. We should be back in S.F. by the end of July or beginning of August at the latest. It should take us between thirty-five and forty-five days to sail Tahiti to S.F. or San Diego direct. It's a long haul, but the cheapest and easiest way. Can't spend anything at sea, you know.

Any time you see any of my friends, tell them I'd like to hear what's going on with them. Perhaps share my last letter. The address is still Poste Restante, Taravao, Tahiti, French Polynesia. You might phone Bruce and ask him if he still has all my power tools. I'll need them when I get back. There is another boat growing in my mind. I just don't know yet where or when it may be built. Perhaps Oregon.

Glad to hear you don't eat wheat anymore. Try millet. It's a complete food, inexpensive, low calorie and not mucous forming. We are even making bread and biscuits out of it with sesame or soy flour. Lay off rice and potatoes and eggs. Get a book by a Dr Arnold Erhard on mucous-less diet from a health food store. Eat lots of fruit and vegetables, kelp, and sesame. It's never to late to clean yourself out. And enjoy yourself in Spain, etc. I'll see you soon.

Love,

Barry

A falling flower
reminds me of the wind
As it blows my way.

Life in the little yellow house

Once we visited the land near the Vaipoiri, we knew what we had to do to in order to make sails out there. As the boat had to be moved to the new 'front yard', we had a fantastic sail from Tapuna Pass to Tahiti-iti. The pass Vaiau was a tricky one that required conning from high up in the rig, but once safely inside the lagoon it was easy to make way into the deep water anchorage in front of the house. Two anchors were set to cover the big swings in wind direction expected during that time of year, and the boat became more like a base than a home. She would sit out there like a loyal pony for the duration of the sail making experiment, waiting for the next part of the voyage.

Rowing ashore for the first time was extra special because you could enter the river from the lagoon and make a landing alongside a big fallen tree sitting at the edge of the river like a perfect dock. This was very much the adventure I had dreamt all my life. What mysteries waited up in the luscious green valley? We were ten kilometers from the end of the road. There would be no cars, not many visitors, and only two neighbors, both kilometers away.

The little yellow house was not in any shape to be used for making sails. It hadn't been lived in for a long time, and wasn't much beyond the floor and a decent tin roof with full sheets of plywood on hinges at the roofline forming all the 'walls'. These walls were almost always propped up with sticks, forming a further extension of the roofline so when it rained, the entire house was still totally open to the outside world. There was a low wall around the floor about a meter high with a bench seat on the inside wall facing the lagoon. Set back about ten meters from the river and the edge of the lagoon, the house stood surrounded by palms and little else. The ground was bare and dry, covered with fallen fronds and all sorts of jungle debris. Between the house and the jungle behind was a patch of grassy level ground that would become the garden. About a hundred feet further along the property was an old storage shack where we could sequester the Honda generator that would power the sewing machine when necessary.

Harlow had some white and yellow paint we could use, and his crew came by to help us with the initial cleaning and preparation. He had permission to take out two walls inside the structure, and this began the opening of our 'loft' in paradise. After all the loose items were removed from the house, we painted the interior walls and floors and left it alone for a few days. That time was spent digging up the garden and planting beans, carrots, lettuce, and radishes, while the dinghy served as the 'dump truck', hauling big flat stones from farther up the river for the path from the river to the house, and to border the garden.

After we were set up to work, I designed the sails and made scale drawings that would allow us to cut the sails in sections of three or four panels. We would do these with rough dimensions, then sew the two or three panel sections together to make the whole sail body.

Once we got into the rhythm of the work, a typical day began with a swim in the river to bathe, an hour of yoga (Patrick was into it too), then a few hours of work on the sails. We'd stop for lunch, which by then had become whatever we could make from our stores on board the *Seminole*. Using our stone-wheel hand grinder we made flour from millet, corn, whole wheat, and rice for pan bread cooked on the Coleman stove. There was also oranges, plantains, bananas, avocado, taro, and other fruits picked up in the valley, as well as tuna, reef crabs, fresh water shrimp, cherry stone clams, and other tasty reef treats to add to the protein level.

Afternoon sail making sessions would always be broken with river swims or jungle walks to look for more food, then we would work into the evening. Sleeping was in the big Mexican hammocks I had on board. We strung them up inside the 'house', and had mosquito nets to cover us from the onslaught. Sometimes in the evening light it was almost surreal to be laying in the hammock, looking out on the boat anchored on the glassy lagoon, thinking, "Wow.... Can this be real?", especially when the canoe full of lovely Tahitian women would come to capture the little clams off the sand bar at the mouth of the river right in front of the house.

Day by day the sections of sails grew to be whole sail bodies. When this was done for the main, mizzen, working jib, stay'sl, and genoa we had a big pile of material all folded tightly into tied up bundles. It would be time for the next step, the big trip to town.

Fortunately we had use of Harlow's 'lagoon car', a sixteen-foot hard bottom inflatable with a twenty-five horsepower outboard. We loaded it up off the riverbank pier and headed across the glass smooth water, scanning always for the nasty coral heads that always seemed to appear out of nowhere and were at best poorly marked with broom sticks or branches. If you weren't careful you could end up stuck high and dry on ragged coral.

When we arrived at the end of the road we were early for the arrival of Le Truck from town. Patrick flagged the driver down and made a deal with him to drop us off at the Cale de Haulage after doing his final stop in town. He would get a case of Hinano for coming and picking us up for the return trip to Teahupo. We loaded all the rough sewn sails onto the roof of the big vehicle along with some pigs in a wire box, two big sacks of copra, and some other large items. An hour later, we were arranging the use of the big lofting floor at the shipyard and getting down to work.

It took relatively little time to get the edges drawn and folded and to draw all the patches and sewing lines. The edges were trimmed and the whole package was folded again and ready for the trip back to the dinghy at the end of the road.

Finishing the rest was the real job and wouldn't require any more trips to town. The small generator provided enough electricity to do the sewing in little one or two hour bursts, and the handwork that went with each sail was done in the total silence of the isolation. We sewed until we were bored, then would swim, hike around, or just do nothing. There was no job I had ever done which was so relaxing and enjoyable.

One of the exciting aspects of this isolated life was the feeling of being some sort of pioneer or adventurer. One day we were far up the valley looking for food when a giant shift in the weather happened, bringing very strong winds and torrential rain to the valley. We stumbled through the jungle to get back to the little house. Managing to stay ahead of the rising water in the stream, we arrived to find the place literally blown around. Inside the house everything was scattered and wet and covered with leaves and fronds blown in with the wind. We shut the plywood panels down and secured everything before heading for the river bank only to find our hard dinghy with the Seagull motor gone, the tree it was tied to ripped from the bank.

THOSE MONTHS WILL LIVE WITH ME FOREVER AS THE MAGIC MOMENTS IN A LIFETIME OF WONDER. By this time it was blowing super hard offshore and the boat was barely visible in the rain. We had to get out there to make sure she was going to be OK, so we put on fins and swam the distance in the rising chop. When we got there the stern was hanging about twenty meters from the coral downwind. We sat there with the engine running hard and steering straight into it until the squall moved on. We had escaped this one, but our dinghy and motor were nowhere to be seen. By this time it was almost dark and we swam ashore and would look for the dinghy another time.

The next morning we walked to Harlow's and got the big RIB and went out along the reef to look for the little boat and motor. Lucky for us we found it floating upside down, motor still attached, and managed a rescue. Lucky again, the rugged Seagull motor cleaned up fine, started up right away and everything was back to normal. Just another day in the jungle.

Those months will live with me forever as the magic moments in a lifetime of wonder. Time was irrelevant and the moments spent with our neighbors and friends served to teach things about life that could have only been learned from such an experience.

*The past cannot dictate the present
and the future cannot be seen.*

Dear Mom,

Just a quick note before we head to town for the last time from our house in paradise. Soon we leave here, probably on Thursday afternoon or evening, to sail back towards Papeete to clear and take stores for the passage back to California. The plan at this moment is to try and sail straight – non-stop from Tahiti to S.F. The only thing which might change is the inclusion of a female crewmember, a beautiful Tahitian woman we admire. God could change our plans too, should he make the winds bad. In either case, we would make a short stop in Hawaii for rest and more fresh stores. We are planning to be back around mid-August.

Life has been exceptionally good to us these last few weeks. I'm making many new friends and really discovering these people and this place. On the winter solstice, we had a nice gathering here. The riverbank was crowded with dinghies and pirogues alike. There were French, Australian, Canadian, American, and Tahitians here all being happy with a sunny day, good food, and music.

We're going to sail out by way of Tahaa, a neighboring island, to look at a piece of land for sale. We've found some folks we like, who want to have someone to share it with them, so we're going to check it out. Cost is about twenty thousand dollars – no cars, no road, and on a bay inside the lagoon, with a white sand beach. Probably much like where we are now.

Another option too. Our neighbor came by for the second time last night to tell us we could come back anytime and live on his land, build a house, etc. He said he loved us, and would like to have us be his neighbor all the time. It's a bit further down the shore from where we are now. It would be the last house on the lagoon, and it's free. That's the way it is here. If they like you, they want you to stay and be their friends. He was almost crying when he told us. All these exchanges are in Tahitian, which I understand and speak more and more each day. I'd like to become fluent before I return.

I intend to return here as soon a possible and would love to live here among all these islands, hopefully to have a place I can call home for a while with a garden, children, dogs and cats; and maybe even a goat and pigs. There is much I can do here to live; building sailing pirogues, fixing clothes, fixing an occasional sail (although I'd like to get away from that as a prime source of livelihood.)

The other day we had a far out thing happen. Some "yachts people" from California came all the way to the end of the road, looking for the sail maker! With them were two sails they wanted me to fix. The women were dressed for the city, make up etc. Fortunately for them, a Tahitian girl in a pirogue saw them (they didn't quite fit the scene, wading through streams and mud to the knees) and gave them a ride in her boat. If they'd walked to our house, they would've had to spend the night! As we were cruising in our dinghy, we met up with them in the lagoon, took the sails, and they went back. What a trip to see these "yachtsmen" out here as they hollered, "Do you know where the sailmaker lives?" Just cracked us up to think of the potential of this place. Those repairs will buy a lot of cheese and honey.

It's time to leave here now though. The people who own our little house want it back. We'll leave it in better shape then when we came, so we can return someday soon. Hope you had a fine trip. Save your money and come to Tahiti next time. You will never want to leave. Who knows, perhaps you wouldn't have to either.

Iorana,

Barry

CHILE RUBBED AHI
WITH FRESH MANGO SALSA

The fruit of one large mango chopped into quarter inch cubes
1 sweet small onion
1 tsp jalapeño peppers canned
Pinch of sea salt
Juice of one line
2 tbls fresh cilantro

Mash altogether to consistency you love.

Take a fresh AHI steak, one inch thick, and rub both sides with dark chili powder.

Heat a tbls butter and 1/2 tbls olive oil in pan till they bubble.
Sear the fish until the ends show that it is cooked both sides.
Squeeze garlic and white wine at the last minute and swirl around.

Place Ahi on plate with mango sauce on top. Serve with fresh manoa lettuce, sliced tomatoes and sliced thin sweet cucumbers. Fresh steamed spinach with a dab of butter, a squeeze of lemon and dash of nutmeg.

Anoint dead tuna!

Dear Mom,

Trying to leave Tahiti as soon as we can. The boat is loaded with stores; fresh, dry, clean and ready to go. We've moved from our little house, and in an evening rain squall, sailed out the pass from the lagoon. It led to a beautiful moonlit sail to Punauia, a few miles from Papeete, where we found a quiet smooth anchorage, very shallow and clear, but close to the road.

The French won't clear my papers for departure until we find Amber or post eleven hundred dollars for her airfare to France. International law says I'm responsible for her, etc. The gendarmes are searching the island for her, as are we, and until she's found and gets off my crew list, we're stuck. Not a bad place to be stuck though. Patrick and I are having a good time playing the bureaucratic games with all these petty bastards. I'm sure the whole thing will straighten itself out as soon as God wills. Right now it's blowing hard N.E., and since that's the direction we want to go it wouldn't be any fun being out there. I'm sure when the wind changes to S.E. or S, everything will be OK.

We'll sail directly to S.F. non-stop, a very long sail but both of us are up for it. Should be thirty-five to forty-five days at sea, less, if we're very lucky. Give us some good thoughts around two to three weeks from now, as we'll be passing through the area of hurricanes. There's one right now called Claudia, good thing we weren't in it as the name is a bit too close. Patrick's ex's name is Diana – I hope she's not waiting there for us!

Hoping to have a beautiful Tahitian woman and her baby come to join me in S.F. She's in France right now, getting ready to go to Morocco. No matter what, I want to come back here and try to buy land on one of the other more remote islands and live for a while before seeing the rest of the world. I am totally in love with this place and its people. See you in August. We'll be sailing in a few days.

Love,
Barry

BARRY SPANIER

This bed is you

And your smell.

Tonite while the moon burns,

Night flowers

Still lie sweet smelling

And I am happy.

Dear Mom,

Short and sweet. Don't worry, I'm fine. I'm not going to New Zealand. Amber is gone - at least today. I'm heading for Hawaii soon. The money deal is not important! Time will take care of everything. I'll find a crew for the trip home. I've worked here some more and made enough to provision. I think Hawaii will open more doors in my life. I'll start a real loft in Lahaina and work there for a while. Long enough to get Claude paid off and build a new boat more suited to my needs.

I'm never idle nor do I waste my talents. Success and failure are all illusions. Inner peace and the love of our fellows is the only thing really worth having. I have my own path. The past cannot dictate the present and the future cannot be seen.

This world of the sea has no guideposts or tracks. Being as free as the wind can be a burden so heavy sometimes I want the permanence offered by a land trip. The burden is the one of constantly having to decide direction. People who are locked into land trips most often don't have to make decisions. They just do the same thing over and over again. I can go anywhere, Fiji, Hawaii, New Zealand, Samoa, Australia – but I have to know why and when. My heart is heavy to let Amber go away, but I know I must. Our love for each other is becoming destructive. Bringing us both down. When time passes, I'm sure I'll look back on it as a lesson learned. That's what already happened once when she went away.

When I get to Hawaii, I'll let you know. I should be here another three weeks or so, twenty to twenty-five days for the passage. Third week in October should do it, God's will. I'll write again before I leave here. My head is sort of empty as I've been working for eighteen days straight, and looking at old rotten sails has burned me out. Also, my emotions have been overworked lately and I feel drained and somewhat lonely. But like a friend of mine says "Every day gets better."

Love you much and hope you don't waste energy with concern for my affairs. My request was not meant to arouse those kinds of feelings. It was simply a request for a loan. Pure business, no expectations. No disappointments.

Love to you and manuia.

Iorana,

Sticks

BIRTHDAY SCALLOPS

Ingredients
1 1⁄2 pound fresh scallops
1 cup sliced fresh mushrooms
1⁄4 cup cut green onions
1⁄2 cup frozen peas (optional)

Sear scallops in butter & olive oil to brown

Add 2 tsp chopped garlic,
1 tsp shredded ginger
1 tble Seafood Magic
1 cup sliced fresh mushrooms

Stir around – add peas.
Add 1⁄4 cup clam juice, 1⁄4 cup white wine

Add a good shot of Thai Sweet Chile sauce

And don't cook the scallops to death!
Two minutes on one side and less on the other.

Serves 4-6 people

*I'm even going to try my hand at making
some clothes from Tahiti flour sacks.
They seem to be quite the style now.*

Dear Mom,

Another note from your wandering son. I'm still in Tahiti but not for long. Early tomorrow morning we will leave here on a brand new adventure. After all the comings and goings and ups and downs and searching my heart, I am now on my way west to see some more of the world in this fine vessel which Claude and I built. Unfortunately, Claude needs something more than *Seminole* and me so I've decided to live my life from now on and will deal with obligations later. Going back to San Francisco was a cop out to the easy way. So you might hear from me in Fiji or New Zealand, not sure just yet. But I'm moving and I'm now heading in that direction.

I am sad not to be able to see the family and I will write more, I promise. Tell Dad I still have the letter I wrote during my decision-making process, but it just never got mailed because it wasn't relevant day to day. Tahiti seems to be a place to make people crazy. It's just all too nice. Read **Blue of Capricorn** by Burdick. It'll give you some idea of what goes on in the minds of travelers in these parts.

I'm healthy, happy, in love with life and living, and ready for whatever happens. I've come to realize more and more, if we don't live each day to its fullest, our lives are soon gone. Years fly by a day at a time and there's no going back. More than anything at this moment, I would like to give you a big hug and see your happy eyes. If you see Claude, tell her I'll write with an explanation as soon as we make our next port. Give my love to all.

Love again,

Sticks

Dear Mom,

Yesterday, a letter I wrote days ago I posted in Bora Bora. It was so many days ago, I can't remember exactly what it said so I'm adding this to it, knowing you'll appreciate hearing more.

Amber and I are sailing this morning to Rarotonga in the Cook Islands, then on to Tonga and New Zealand. There, I'll work on *Seminole*; haul, paint, etc. and perhaps work to earn some money.

I'd like to go north to New Hebrides and New Guinea, perhaps next year. I'm doing this for myself – and not going back to Hawaii. I'm taking the step to the unknown for once – no jobs waiting, no friends – just a new land and new adventures. I'm terribly excited, a little scared sometimes, but ready to let it flow.

These last months have been good to me, a freedom I can't explain. I'm sure now I'll write more often and hope I can hear from you once in awhile. I would say you could use 'Captain of the Port, Opua, New Zealand' as an address. That would be better, and before I get there I'll write from Rarotonga or Tonga. I'm kind of in a hurry this morning because we'd like to leave in a few hours. Much work to do to be ready for sea. Too bad about Hawaii... but I just couldn't go back. Not yet.

Maybe you'll make it to New Zealand? Should be nice there this summer.

Love you always,

Barry

I had to go.

To look.

To see if it was a dream.

To have the loneliness

And the time

To talk to myself.

To wish someone was there to dream with me.

Even if it wasn't right,

The dream wouldn't go away.

The need to float,

Free.

To wake to sounds of lying at anchor,

To breathe stars,

To become the sky,

So full of them.

When a soul is touched by the sea,

Its heart can never forget

And only seeks that peace.

Dear Mom,

What? Another letter from your wandering son so soon? To what do we owe this? You know I only seem to write when there is some news, so here's the news.

I sailed from Papeete to Hua'hine and Bora Bora with my crazy French lady. That much you should already know. They were days of joy, peace and happiness, loving in the sun and living each moment intensely. We had a fine passage from Bora Bora to Rarotonga, five days of easy sailing, good weather and seemingly mutual enjoyment.

Here in Rarotonga, Amber did an about face, suddenly hating me and everything about me. Our life together disintegrated in hours. I've seen it happen before, the same way several times, and it now leads me to believe she is really troubled, crazy that is. Paranoid schizophrenic, almost psychotic sometimes, and quite violent. We fought again physically after she attacked me. She is no longer going to be with me; my choice as much as hers. It seems, even if I give her all my love, she will never know how to accept it without feeling trapped. It is with a mixture of sadness and gladness I see her go, and I now know it is still my choice to sail westward and try a new country again.

So I'm alone again, this time in a place I must leave by October 19, no maybes. There is little hope of finding a crew by then, as it is a small place with no yachts and few people traveling, so there is a good chance I'll be sailing single-handed to New Zealand, perhaps direct, or stopping at Tonga Tapu, about nine hundred miles west of here. I had plenty of practice sailing the boat nearly alone with Amber as she did not understand sailing at all. She loved being on the boat and at sea, which seemed to make up for it. However, when it came to working the boat, changing sails, etc, I was doing most of it by myself anyway. We were fortunate to have good weather, so the practice was easy.

I must leave this area soon. The hurricane season rapidly approaches, and I have no desire to encounter any storm such as this. New Zealand should offer up summer weather and hopefully is a friendly place for work opportunity and getting the *Seminole* in good shape. I actually welcome my aloneness and feel it is a good thing for my concentration on the problems at hand. I may even be able to sell her there for a fair price and square up that part of my life too. Right now, no plans for the future, just do what I must do for now. Fix the stove, repair some sailing gear, clean the boat, and buy stores for the passage.

If I go to Tonga Tapu, I intend to approach their government about work as a consultant for sail making and maintenance. I would be willing to teach the Tongans how to build and maintain sails for their proposed sailing merchant vessel, which is supposed to be under construction. It's a wild stab but could work. One never knows until one tries.

I'm even going to try my hand at making some clothes from Tahiti flour sacks. They seem to be quite the style now. I invested some money in them and have quite a few onboard right now.

So have no fears for me, only good positive thoughts and as soon as I get somewhere you can write, I'll let you know. I haven't had mail for so long, I feel sort of separated. Perhaps you will be able to visit me somewhere 'down under', who knows. Give my love to the grand folks and put them at ease.

Affectionately and with love,

Barry

BARRY SPANIER

Dear Mom,

Everything is certainly safe and sound. I left Rarotonga with Amber still on board. The Raro immigration wouldn't let her off the boat unless she had lodging, tickets, etc., so she said she'd sail to TongaTapu with me. We even patched up our differences. I also found a twenty year-old fellow from New Zealand off another boat. He wanted to get back home. His name is Michael Smith and he's a sailmaker at a Hood loft in Auckland. We have much to talk about and when I get there I should have some help getting work. He's an experienced sailor and I trust him.

I want to try and relay some of my last three weeks. The passage from Raro was uneventful and easy although we had light headwinds a good part of the way. Arrived in Tonga Tapu on Halloween and so far have found it to be a fine place with friendly people. We spent the first few days engaged in "business" which I'll tell you of later. About six days ago, with Michael staying on the boat, Amber and I took a small ferryboat to a neighboring island, Eua. It's a volcano, very young geologically, and has the finest cross section of life I've seen in the Pacific. The people are extremely poor, but the land is good with forests, rivers, high grassy plateaus, and jungle filled with colorful birds.

First day: Arrived in the village of Ohonua and were met by Liuaki Fungalei, a teacher at Hofanga Hau College, really more like a junior high school. We met him in Nukuolofa earlier through another young man, Sifa, a student of his. Liu and Sifa went with us to a picnic on a beautiful stretch of coastline on the weather side of Eua. We played and talked all day with the forty or so students who were to begin the Tongan government higher living exams this week. They were genuinely curious about what we knew and felt about the world. They have few books and no school supplies but still study and learn somehow. Most speak some English, some quite well. The teachers really care about what they're doing and are trying to update the curriculum to modern standards, of course at odds with an administration that is still in the 1920's.

Lunch came out of the ground from an umu with hot rocks and banana leaves, food buried inside all day. Mutton, yams, taro, manioc, and umara. All the people sat in a row along an organic setting. There were palm fronds and the banana leaves from the oven, food on the leaves. A long singing chanting grace, then everybody dove in. All were eating and talking when suddenly about twenty people stood up quickly and walked away without a word. The boys explained it is a custom; when you are quite satisfied with the meal you leave the table so as to not eat more than you need. Even though they eat starchy vegetables and pork, they are generally quite trim.

That evening, Amber stayed on the beach with two young women from the village while I went back to the college and spoke with the men. We had a fine evening comparing values and experience. They want to know and grow but don't have the tools. I'm going to give you the names and addresses of the school for your sorority ladies. If they'd like to help some independent children for a change, have them send a carton of clothing and especially books and school supplies to this place. Books should be non-fiction, classics, science or technical. They will certainly have more value than the nickels and dimes they bring to your rummage sale. They especially need to know about nutrition and hygiene.

WHAT A JOY TO BE WITH PEOPLE WHO STILL KNOW HOW TO LIVE WITH EACH OTHER AND LAUGH AND SING TOGETHER.

The next morning I walked back into the forest with a young man and spent several hours in pleasant conversation. These people have such a fine way about them and are filled with hope for a good future. He hoped to pass his exams and go on to two years of high school and perhaps a university in Fiji or N/Z. Later in the day, I walked back about six miles to Ohonua, through village after village of friendly people. I met Amber there and we spent the night on a fine beach just out of the village.

The next morning, we went to church with our newly adopted Tongan family, all in Tongan dress. A clean white shirt for me with a wrap around skirt of woven grass tied with a human hair belt around my waist. Very elegant. Amber was all in blue silk with the same type of grass mat around her waist. This is a custom to show respect for the King and your parents.

After church, as the honored guests, we had a Sunday meal cooked in umu, with octopus, sea snails, fish, crab, and beef. The core of the feast was a pig that had been walking around the afternoon before. It was topped off with some vegetables, still no fruit. It seemed strange to have days without fruit in a place where it should be everywhere. But it isn't cultivated or harvested because they have white flour and sugar, which is easier. The root crops grow practically wild so there is little effort required to get them. When it comes to eating, they use little of what they have, preferring cans and flour to natural foods. One older man I spoke to at length said when he was a young man (he is now sixty-four) there were many men and women in their eighties and nineties. Now they seldom make seventy. I asked him why, and he said it was because people ate white flour, sugar and canned stuff; not the healthy Tongan foods. He said he only ate Tongan food and looked very good for it, still with black hair and a lean strong body.

The Sunday meal was in the remains of our "family's" old house; the corner posts, roof beams, and foundation being over two hundred years old. The old man told us when Captain Cook came to Eua in 1776 for two days, he had taken kava there and eaten in that house. That night Amber and I slept there, the roof now gone, just the stars overhead.

We spent the rest of our island stay with these people, helping around, walking about, living and eating with them. The Sunday afternoon, we rode some incredibly bony horses, bareback, to the forestlands high on the island exploring caves, grottos and enjoying grand views from the hilltops.

The next day, the family put on a kava ceremony for the village elders where we were invited to participate and given Euan ceremonial names. I'm NoFonua and Amber is Jopokoro. These are names we will use in any kava drinking we do in Tonga so people will know we're from Eua. Having had a good deal of experience with psychedelic drugs, I find kava to be mildly like a psychedelic, making you quiet, contemplative with altered time sense and aural and visual perception. Very much better than the alcohol cultures now found in the other islands we've been to. Following the kava, we had another umu feast with a freshly killed pig, yams and taro, followed with more kava and a nice nap.

On Tuesday, Amber, nineteen year-old Mafi, and I went to a waterfall and jungle high behind the "college", explored a deep cave in the mountain and enjoyed eating mangoes, coconuts, and wild lemons all day. We were then home that evening in time for a party we dreamt up. It was an impromptu theater and dance thing with Amber and I as the 'stars'. We made a mask from the hipbones of a cow we found on our walk, used the lower jaws of a horse, some cardboard and Spanish moss, dyed with tapa dye. It was a wolf for sure. I was the wolf, Amber was Little Red Riding Hood, Mafi the Woodsman, and Langakali, 16, the Grandma. Fifty or sixty village children, one Coleman lamp, wild laughter, and great times. They made us do the play three times. We sang and danced to radio or guitars, theatre style till late at night. What a joy to be with people who still know how to live with each other and laugh and sing together. No T.V. or disco bullshit turning their heads to mush. Too many times in Tahiti or the other Societies, even when there was no electricity you'd see ten or twelve people wordlessly watching some pablum in the darkness, the tube running off a car parked close by. All sitting, staring, giving their souls to the "Eye".

On Eua, even though everyone's clothes were tired and old, the cupboard had only oil, salt and sugar, and there was no money, there was still a joy and singing happiness from within.

The next morning after a breakfast of lobster and yams, I went back to Nukua'lofa, leaving Amber, who'll return Saturday. She wanted to stay and watch them make tapa and coconut oil and weave the fine baskets and mats they make. This place has the finest crafts I've seen.

Now my plans. Today I'm going to talk to Peter Warner, an Australian ship owner who is interested in having a commercial sized sailing vessel to work between Australia and American Samoa, using a Tongan crew. A week ago I talked with him for several hours about his project and expressed my interest in his ideas. Today I'm going to more forcefully offer my services in the hope of some connection in the fairly near future. I'm going to see the King of Tonga about teaching Tongans sailmaking, or at least getting someone skilled to work here. They have many local boats that still use only sail power and have no trained sail makers in all these one hundred islands. I have an open proposal in mind and will give it a try.

After that's done, a short trip to some of the northern islands, perhaps ten to fourteen days and then to New Zealand, for boat maintenance, earn some money, and change my lifestyle a bit. I feel like I'm planting many seeds now and need to give them time to grow. I want to see Mark Switzer and his place on Great Barrier Island. He should be in NZ around December.

Now the explanation about the money. In Tahiti, I lent over four hundred dollars to two friends. I expect to be greeted in New Zealand with letters containing the funds, but right now I have nothing. Not quite nothing. I have sixty New Zealand dollars in ten dollar bills, which for some reason I cannot change into Tongan money even at the bank. Some NZ law about removing currency from the country, unknown to me before. My crew is broke as well, and I like to keep totally independent of Amber when it comes to money because all of our fights seem to start over a few dollars. When we stay clear with each other money-wise, our lives together are really quite wonderful. Besides, I'm not sure whether she will sail to NZ with me, or stay here, or go on to Fiji. I don't want to depend on her in any way. Also, this place has so many fine crafts, and I'd like to get some things to send to you. They're so inexpensive, but with only thirteen Tongan dollars, I can't even think of it. So if you sent the money, it will be well used and appreciated and I'll return it as soon as I find some work in NZ.

So that's where I am now. It costs nearly nothing to live here. Two pounds of tomatoes for ten cents, a five pound cabbage for forty cents, melons twenty cents each, ten green peppers for ten cents, carrots and cucumbers five cents a pound, and cheese and butter fifty cents a pound. Only the cans and imported food is dear. Thirty pounds of sweet potatoes for two dollars. We have everything we need to have a healthy life on about a dollar a day for two people. And we receive many gifts from the people of fruit and coconuts. So life is good and staying simple. No drinking, little smoking, no dope, and a clear head for the future.

I'll drop a note before we leave for NZ and let you know how we're doing. Give my best to all, perhaps you can share this letter with everyone.

Love to you,

Barry

Ahhhhh.
Yes.
Formed as sound,
open,
round,
inviting.
Even followed by sweet serpent sssssssss,
still beckoning.

Meanwhile.... No...
starts with tongue
closed against the palate,
shut off,
hard,
dragging you down the moldy hall.
past the dark empty rooms,
slammed into the stairwell
at the end.
Red exit sign
changing your colors.
The lone sax player in 314
blowing cool red
into blue.

No's ok.
Always another day.

Aloha

November 25, 1977
Nukualofa, Tonga

Dear Mom,

Leaving tomorrow sometime for NZ... just Michael and I, the young fellow I picked up in Rarotonga. Amber is moving off today. It's sort of like a fire all burned out. Too much for both of us to take. Love, but it just isn't worth the hassles. No hard feelings, just apathy.

So we look to about eleven hundred miles of what should be good sailing. It's been blowing hard NE for the last week or so, and strong N around NZ, good weather for going south. We will enter and clear at Opua, from there I don't know. Perhaps Christmas I'm at Great Barrier Island with Mark Switzer (I've enclosed a letter for him. Could you deliver it – 2714 Hyde St and say hello?) I got your gift and will airfreight a return gift for you as soon as I arrive in NZ. I'm going to boldly spend the extra you sent. I'm sure you'll be pleased at the return. Even if it's late for Christmas it should always brighten your house and your life. There will be some things for the folks too.

I'm kind of in a hurry to get this posted so I won't get very strung out. Tonga is a beautiful place and you also have a family here now. You will be welcome with Foeta and Katalina should you ever travel here. Hotels are cheap. Transport too. And food is extra low priced. You may even receive a gift from them around Christmas. I really love those people and their children and hope you can meet them someday.

Hope you had a nice Thanksgiving and that everyone is healthy and happy.

All my love,

Barry

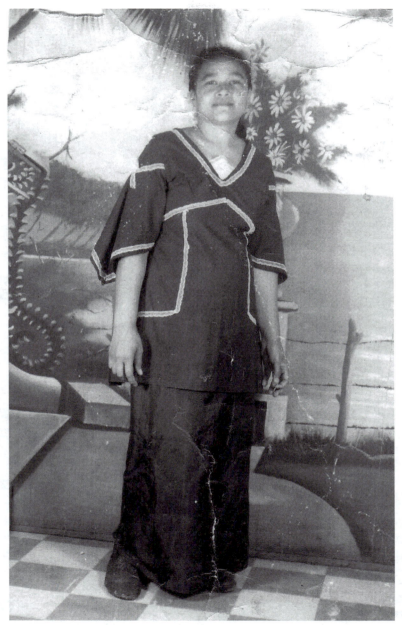

Katalina Takai 1977

NEW ZEALAND

BARRY SPANIER

Dear Mom,

After a fast passage of nine days from Tonga, we arrived safely two days ago. We were aided by winds of forty to fifty knots from the NE as a tropical cyclone named Steve came down on us from the north. Three days of gale force winds and breaking seas; followed by twelve hours of eerie calmness, two more days in a westerly gale, and a couple of days of light headwinds and clear weather to the finish.

There are just two of us on board with Amber staying behind in Tonga. I don't know what our future will be, but I intend to try and be with her again. It's our present needs which keep us apart. She needs to play and I need to work on the boat, earn money and sell the boat soon. I'm going to Auckland to attempt all this. Then I'll probably return to the Bay of Islands to finish the maintenance and work. I'm going to send you a parcel, airfreight so it will arrive around Xmas. I'll enclose a note with it, explaining all.

This place is truly beautiful. Lots of islands and inlets in a giant bay, well protected with warm weather, good wind, and gentle countryside. Not having been here long I can't really tell much of the people, but the first impression is they are friendly but quite conservative. It feels like Oregon fifteen years ago.

There are many 'freaky' young people and commune folks because of the country atmosphere. City flee'ers. But older people, shopkeepers, officials, etc., are very uptight. I have a beard again and my hair is several inches below my shoulders and almost white blond. With my hand sewn clothes, I guess I stand out some so I should expect to be treated strangely. Funny though, in Tonga, Tahiti and the other places we've been, although the people are naturally curious, they don't prejudge. Western minds now seem to be so closed and narrow.

I've written to several friends to try and sell the boat. Tell whoever you want - she is for sale, everything goes, no bargaining. She will be hauled, repainted and essentially ready to go.

Sorry this letter can't be more cheery. It really doesn't reflect my state of mind, which is really very elevated and together. I'm alone on the boat now, going day sailing today with a friend from Tahiti and a couple of pretty Australian women. I'm eating lightly but well, doing yoga, not drinking, and haven't smoked joints for a long time. Mostly I'm happy. I sorely miss Amber but who knows, she may miss me too. Absence makes the heart etc.....

I think you'll appreciate the value and quality of the crafts I purchased for you in Tonga. I intend to go back there and spend more time with those people. Don't forget my family. You know you'd be an honored guest in their humble home should you ever decide to travel in the South Pacific. I sure hope you do. Friends have arrived, must close.

Love,

Barry

BARRY SPANIER

December 1977

Cruising into Westhaven Harbour in Auckland on a foggy early morning, Mike Smith and I looked for a likely side tie. A guy in foulies walked up the dock, took our dock lines and told us we would be OK in the most logical spot. He introduced himself as Geoffrey Bourne. Tea was in order.

When we got to talking, we found we had come close to meeting while we were both in Tahiti, but always just missed. He said he heard stories about the sailmaker and sort of knew of me. We chatted for a good while and he offered what advice he had, based on being there a few weeks longer than me. Getting work, getting hauled, and where to eat out is all the news you need. Before he left, he told me about the crowd at Marsden Wharf, and the Whitbread Round-the-world Race vessels, where work might be a possibility. It was worth a try. After a quick trip under power, we were tied to the pier right behind Skip Dashew's Columbia 52 and across from the most advanced ocean racing yachts of the day.

But there was no work. Each boat had its own sailmaker grunt and they did nothing but work on the sails and rig. Nothing for me there.

One afternoon Iris Macia climbed down the ladder and came aboard. We hadn't been together since Tahiti. She was working as a nurse, had a comfortable home, and was always in the mood to help a sailor. She fed me, let me have a good hot bath, and thoroughly enjoyed my company. When she dropped me back to the *Seminole,* there was an invitation to her big Christmas Day party, including a ride to and from the party. That girl loved her sailors.

Faithful to the invite, she came and got me Christmas Day. This was a wonderful interlude from the rest of what was going on (no food shopping, no wine or beer, alone on Christmas Eve). The first person I saw when entering Iris's house was Geoffrey, looking a bit wild eyed and probably having some sort of extra-legal fun. The rest of the crowd was all from Iris's work life, or fellow pub crawlers. Considering Geoff's mindset, and as Iris was chasing some other guy, I didn't stay long. As I was leaving, Geoffrey suggested we take *Seminole* out to the watch the start of the next leg of the big race, planned for Boxing Day, December 26th. That sounded fine to me.

Geoffrey turned up on time and quickly showed he was an able hand. His years of experience included delivering a boat from San Diego to the Caribbean, his position as mate on the Berlusconi's *Alpha Centauri* from the West Indies to Tahiti, and various rides from Tahiti to New Zealand. Everything he owned was in his backpack, and he knew the way around my rig as if he'd been working the *Seminole* for years.

After the race started, I suggested we peel off and head for Waiheke Island, also known as 'the land of the unwed mum', a tidy little place with almost no men, and many perfect places to anchor with good protection. Geoffrey was all for it, and unknown to us, it would be the beginning of a lifetime partnership in business and as friends.

We wandered Waiheke but didn't find anything interesting to keep us there. Back to the boat for dinner and sleep seemed more rewarding, especially after the day's sailing. About two in the morning a rising breeze woke me. There was a huge moon making the little bay's waters glisten and sparkle. Geoffrey came on deck at almost the same time and suggested going sailing, so without much further discussion we decided on the next goal, an anchorage to the north. We stowed to be underway again, raised the anchor, set sail, and headed out the bay.

What followed was days of adventure and camaraderie that took us to one cool place after another. It became such an easy sharing of the responsibilities of the boat and I developed complete trust in the ability of my new shipmate. We had no set watches scheduled but it always seemed to work out that one of us was prepared to be alert so the other could rest. We fished and ate good, shared cooking and cleaning, and generally just had a gas. The journey evolved as we went north and I was happy with the idea of making it back to Opua in the Bay of Islands for New Years eve. That led us to the *Constellation*, and our lengthy work trip as 'partners'.

Geoffrey and I would end up forming a real business partnership in Maui, working together with faith and trust for twenty years, and today we are still 'partners' in the true sense where that means friends for life, always willing to help each other as much as possible. Over those years we each stood watch for each other in so many respects. A voyage of sorts, with great success and many more of those good times along the way.

BARRY'S SALMON WITH PERSIMMON, HONEY AND KOMBU GLAZE

1 or 2 salmon fillet with the skin
1 whole ripe persimmon
1 leaf kombu seaweed
2 tbls honey
1/2 cup white wine
Cayenne pepper
2 tbls olive oil

Lightly sprinkle the skin side of the salmon fillet with powdered cayenne (amount depends on your wuss factor). Cook at a medium heat with the skin side down and lid on pan until fish is starting to get cooked through. Then flip the fish over and cook at higher heat to sear the topside. After a minute or two, take the fish off, put on a plate with the skin side down.

Scoop insides out of a ripe persimmon. Cook in salmon pan with honey and wine. Rinse the kombu, pat dry and cut into 1/2 inch long thin strips (like little black worms) and cook them in the salmon pan until all ingredients get a glazy look about them. Then pour over the salmon fillets.

Serve with steamed fresh beet slices. This adds a sweet flavor to compliment the taste of the salmon and besides the color looks good. Garnish with Italian parsley, cilantro, whatever. It's something you can eat.

Dear Mom,

Nice morning, with some sun for a change. The boat is in the center of the city, tied at Marsden Wharf, along with a dozen or so sixty to seventy-five foot international yachts of the racing variety. They're here for the layover before the second leg of the Whitbread Round theWorld Race from Auckland to Rio – about seven thousand miles. This wharf is now a multi-lingual sailing event. In a couple of days, we're going to sail to a small island a few hours from here and spend a few days. The 'we' is now Steve Grey, a twenty-five year old fellow from Minnesota, who's been bumming around the Pacific for a year or so.

I've been taking advantage of the city, going to hear free concerts and jazz music. Checking on haul out possibilities but won't be able to do anything until I get some money together. Absolutely want to sell the boat. I have around four hundred dollars owed to me and am trying to sell some things that are worth about sixty dollars. Right now, I've got nine dollars to my name and getting away from the city is imperative.

The photograph enclosed is Katalina Takai, my Tongan 'mother'. It belongs in the center of the tapa with her name on it. She made it special for Amber and I. The other tapas come from various markets in Tonga. The larger soft one was a blanket in a home for a while. You may cut it up if you wish, to get it to a size for wall hanging. Tapa is very expensive in the U.S. but cheap in Tonga. Maybe Ernie could cut it cleverly to get the most out of it. The other tapas are for the family. You might see that Dad and Veronica get one, the folks, and Ernie and M.R. The two baskets are for you as well as the shells and whatever tapa you want.

I'm glad to hear of what you're doing for the people at the school and for my/our family. I wouldn't be surprised if they didn't send you something as well.

I've been meeting some very fine people here in NZ, who are into simple living in the countryside, doing alternative trades. There are apparently large numbers; so many, the country may see the planet survive down this way.

This next month here should be interesting. I feel more like in a waiting state than I have in a long while. I intend to be patient and calm because there is not much I can do just this moment. I have a couple of sail making jobs lined up but they are 'maybe' still. I could've worked for a large factory-type loft, but it was night work only and terrible pay. It's better if I put energy into the boat than work for two dollars an hour.

There is nothing I need seriously. I don't wear glasses anymore. Amber made me stop. I have everything else I need. If I need clothes, I can make them. I have a good deal of material. I just need a buyer for the boat.

I'm going to close for now. I don't know if this'll make it by Xmas but I'll say Merry Merry anyway. Many thanks for the extra money in Tonga. Like I said before, it's returning in crafts. I think often of you and the folks, and always hope you are healthy and happy.

Love,

Barry

December 19, 1977
Auckland

Dear Mom,

I suppose I shouldn't have been so naïve to think shipping the things I bought for you would be easy. Or relatively inexpensive.

First, the basket is a beautiful woven piece with a lid twenty-four inches in diameter and twenty-six inches tall. But even loaded with the shells, tapa and other things, it only weighs about twenty pounds. So it goes by the minimum rate for surface freight, about ninety dollars including customs (not duty, just filling out all the paperwork). Airfreight would be around two hundred dollars because it is a large, light thing.

Soooo.... Here's what I'm going to do. Sadly, I'm going to hang on to all of those things in the hopes I'll find someone who's flying back to the states who can take it as baggage. Or, when I get the money, I'll ship it surface freight, or, if the boat sells, I'll be shipping a large quantity of goods, tools, etc. and I can send it then.

Really is too bad, as these things are very beautiful and I did so want you to have them for Christmas. I'm going to check with a friend who is an airline pilot. Perhaps something will work out.

No matter what happens, know I'm trying and my heart is with you, even if my presents can't be.

Love,

Barry

WOULDN'T WHIP NO MORE BEETS

One large beet
1 to 1 1/2 cup of water
Juice of half a lime
2 tbls plain yogurt
1 tsp nutmeg

You can skin the beet if you want. I'm lazy; I scrub them and eat them; besides all the good stuff is in the outside. Trim the tentacles and cut the stem out. Then cut it up into thick chunks and cook in about a cup or cup and half of water, slowly till the water's about half gone. Not really simmering, just low temperature so they cook a while and the water gets stinky red. Then pull the beets out and heat the water a little bit and add the lime juice and nutmeg, then whip the yogurt in until it's emulsified. Then pour it over the beets with a piece of tarragon. However, we were missing it cuz we're a tarragon free household.

Serve it with fresh ahi (tuna) in sashimi style with ginger

Dear Mom,

Getting ready for a trip south to the Coramandel Peninsula for a three-day music festival. Got an offer of two good jobs, one refitting a seventy-six foot Schooner and the other working for a fellow building a one hundred ten foot steel ketch. Either job pays well and will be satisfying calling on all my skills as a boat builder and sail maker. So I'm happy and together, and have a good mate, Geoff, a twenty-seven year-old American, and a new friend Marianne, a young NZ woman. Good companions.

Hope this all arrives in good order. John is a good fellow to bring this stuff with him. A great savings. You might be able to do something for him.

Love,

Barry

Dear Mom,

We're sailing in a light easterly breeze with a big NE swell. We're going from Mayor Island in the Bay of Plenty, east of the Coramandel Peninsula, heading for Tauranga with Marianne, Geoff, and two NZ dairy farmers we picked up on the island who invited us to have a look at their farms.

This last week and a half we've been sailing from Russell to here. We leave an anchorage around mid-day, sail until dark, find a cozy hole, anchor, eat, sleep, and then sail in the sun again. We're hiking and climbing naked through the trees, and over grassy slopes. The purpose was a pre-work time exploration of New Zealand and to attend a three-day music and crafts festival at Golden Valley, near Waihi. It's been incredibly good sailing, much going to weather, and varied conditions. It's been hard work, but good for me to feel so fit.

Mayor Island is a wildlife reserve crisscrossed with incredibly rugged footpaths that wind in and out of a densely forested crater with two lakes at the bottom, one green and one black as coal. We climbed and tramped all through the place, blown away by the amazing bird life and richness of the forest.

I must say the last four weeks of my life have been the most rewarding and true learning experience I've had in many years. Intense sailing and a new feeling of confidence and faith in the boat and my own abilities.

I have work for at least one and a half months when I return to Russell with potential for much more. The job is a complete refit on *Constellation*, a 76'

Alden staysail schooner, built in 1932. Geoff and I are going to rebuild the main mast, re-rig the boat, repair woodwork and sails, and refinish all her exterior. We got good terms for work and excellent pay. I could earn more making sails, but would rather do this first because the '*Connie*' is such a fine old lady and needs help.

I gave your package to a young man named John, an Australian merchant seaman. He said he'd be in L.A. around the first week in February, and in Oakland around the twelfth or the thirteenth. He'll phone you from L.A., and then when he gets to Oakland. You will have to go pick it up. He's young and rowdy so I don't know what you could do for him, short of a fine thanks and maybe a jug of good rum.

My Tongan family has all sizes; you couldn't send anything too big or too little. And never fear it wouldn't find it's way to another 'relative' somehow. As I said before, if you went to Tonga, my family would make you an honored guest for any time you spent with them. But I have to warn you, as far as Tongan traveling goes, it's very primitive but it would be so rewarding. They speak and read English somewhere in the village.

New Zealand is an amazing and beautiful place. Natural and friendly people. You'd dig it, real clean and together. I plan to leave here by mid-May for somewhere, and figure to be working heavily until then.

Amber wrote and said she's mad to be with me and wants to come to NZ. I wrote and told her to come here. Some way we'll be together.

My food is decent if I cook for myself. Restaurants are relatively expensive and not so good. But market food quality is high and prices fair.

I weigh about 165, I'm strong and brown all over, bearded again, my hair is blonde and several inches below my shoulders. I never wear my glasses anymore. Sunglasses either. My eyes are getting stronger. There are times when I strain to see, but when I don't try, I seem to see better. My eyes now look strong, not all white and small and weak from hiding all the time.

I'm going to need some parts for haul out and some minor repairs I won't be able to get here. Just small stuff. If I send a list, could you go to WHE and get it? It should happen fairly soon.

Will you run an ad in the Chron? One full week.
>   38' Atkin Ingrid, Cutter Rig, Diesel.
>   Must sell Ph 731 5190 Eves for info.

I spread the word here through friends and bulletin boards but I think it's pretty hopeless. Best results seem to be from letters to California. I want to avoid brokers and boat hustlers.

Let me know on my requests and I'll get on my end of it here.

Thanks and love,

Barry

GO WITH WHAT YOU GOT

THE *CONSTELLATION*

What a fine voyage it turned out to be. All night there were pods of dolphins breathing alongside, white caps everywhere, and a million stars.

The *Constellation* limped into New Zealand just ahead of the *Seminole*. She had a dead generator and main engine. She was a sitting duck for bad weather, being manned only by Chris Heg and the owner's eighteen year old son, Poindexter Erb (for real!). The sails and running rigging were a mess, and the anchor windlass was barely functional, so they would have been in serious danger had there been any drastic change in the conditions.

After setting our anchor and before heading to town, we rowed by the *Constellation* and had a gam with the young guys to find out what was going on with the boat. We'd been sailing for two days, coming non-stop from Whangerei, and were looking forward to getting a hot shower and a beer. New Years was coming soon, and the town of Russell was filling with young people and families on vacation. The fruit trees had some good picking too.

After finding a friendly shower stall at a local boat yard, we wandered into the Duke of Marlboro pub and found it full of crazy-drinking Aussie tourists, mostly young guys with ten or fifteen plastic beer cups stacked up like a tower, adding to each one with a new full cup, the challenge being to not spill the lot. There were some really long arms that afternoon, and the whole show was giving us an idea of what we could expect for New Years.

Being in town for a week, we met a lot of young people around the Duke. Among them were a number of pretty girls, and through Dexter and Chris, we also met a number of young guys. Once we cleaned up the *Seminole* and put her to sleep safely we had little to do during the days. It left plenty of time for exploring the small town, finding all the fruit trees and vegetable gardens, as well as creating some 'recreational diversions'. In other words, we were looking to party.

New Years was crazy. New Zealand had pub laws which said closing was 10:00 P.M. on weekdays and 11:00 on Saturday nights. There was an exception for New Years to allow them to stay open to 12:30. The Duke was packed. Inside it was shoulder to shoulder and got crazier and crazier as the night went on. Guys who were too drunk to stand found themselves in the rafters, and as the clock approached midnight they pissed on the crowd below. Needless to say this caused an upset, and soon there was a lot of beer and glasses flying around the room. We decided to beat a hasty retreat, helping some nice Aussie girls to escape before the police and fire department came to clear out the crowd. We took them sailing on New Years day.

Geoffrey and I grew bold about visiting the *Constellation* and worked at encouraging the two young guys to get her in shipshape and capable of being sailed in an emergency. Every day, we met more young people in the bars and on the street, and soon we had a regular crew coming every day to help out. It wasn't long before we began to ease Dexter and Chris into going along with doing a sailing trip. After all, Roberta, Dexter's mother, wouldn't be back for weeks. What would be the harm?

There was a local yacht race that gave us a good excuse to get the adventure rolling. We stocked up on beer and food at the expense of our 'crew', and made 'up anchor' a community job for the ten others on board (the windlass was toast). As we fell away from the anchorage, we hoisted the staysail and foresail and got our steerage away. We had just succeeded in 'borrowing' this wonderful old yacht for some fun. Soon the main was up, and then the big genoa. It didn't take long to get her fifty-five tons rolling across the bay towards Cape Brett, the headland that guards the South side of the entrance to the Bay of Islands. Within hours we were sailing down the coast looking for a friendly anchorage.

Our crew was almost completely inexperienced, so Geoffrey and I took the role of teachers, and we got them all into scrubbing, rubbing, and washing even while we were underway. The old girl was looking better by the hour. And the kids were getting lessons in sail handling, tacking, and a little navigation. Our charts showed a deep little bay about ten miles down the coast, so we decided to head in and find a place to anchor for the night.

With the main engine dead, and the wind light and getting lighter as we got closer to the shore, we lowered the hard bottom inflatable with the twenty-five horse outboard, hooked the dinghy alongside tugboat style, and pushed the *Constellation* into the bay. The only issue was getting a good set on the anchor without a lot of power, but this little cove was so protected we really weren't worried.

And what a place it was. We were in about fifteen feet of crystal blue water, with a high shore very close. There was a small waterfall close enough to hear, and it fell into a big pool that was elevated above the tide line, big enough for almost all the crew to frolic around.

There was a decent trail to the top of the land and we explored the plateau. There were several plum trees, apples, and a wall of blackberries just getting ripe. We didn't see any people and took it as a good sign these fruit trees were there just for us.

We swam and laid around in the afternoon sun, hiked around the bay, harvested mussels, oysters, and dug those little clams they call 'pippies' from a small sand beach nearby. Our dinner was well covered by our trip to nature's 'store'. This crew of newbies was getting the idea fast. One can live well when floating.

Once our food ran out, especially the beer, we had to think about getting back to Opua/Russell to make sure the *Constellation* was safe on her mooring. Using the inflatable again, we 'tug-boated' out of the little bay and set sail north-bound for the Bay of Islands. It would probably be an overnighter, so there was some excitement about that on board.

What a fine voyage it turned out to be. All night there were pods of dolphins breathing alongside, white caps everywhere, and a million stars. The old girl slid along doing eight or nine knots effortlessly, and all on board had one of those once-in-a-lifetime great sails.

WHEN THE SOUL IS TOUCHED BY THE SEA, ITS HEART CAN NEVER FORGET AND ONLY SEEKS THAT PEACE.

Dawn took us around Cape Brett and we were ghosting along inside the Bay of Islands again. *Seminole* was still holding the same spot, and in a short time our chain was rumbling through the hawse pipe too. We had done it. We did the round trip without engine, no problems. The crew cleaned her up, and we all went ashore for a beer in the pub.

Fate was kind to us because Roberta, (Roberta Candler Erb) the owner of the *Constellation*, arrived back in New Zealand the next afternoon. The boat was so clean and ship-shape she knew something had been going on. (I had cleaned her cabin so she really knew.) She quickly drew the best part of the story out of her son (he kept the sailing part to himself, thank goodness!) and she couldn't figure out whether to be mad or happy the boat was in such good shape.

In the end, she came to Geoffrey and asked him if he would take charge of the giant re-fit and re-construction project. He said he would agree on the condition I would be his 'foreman' and run the boat-building part of the job. It began five months of the most challenging work we could have ever imagined, which generated the money necessary for me to get the *Seminole* back in shape and ready for sea again.

GO WITH WHAT YOU GOT

Three small bolts secured each band and as the bolts were removed we began to hear lots of cracking and creaking noises, as though some spirit was trying to escape after years of bondage.

THE "*CON*" INSTALLATION

The more you know, the less you have to fear.

After the deal was made to manage the rebuild of the *Constellation*, we accompanied her down the coast to Tauranga and settled her into the boatyard. Geoffrey and I were going to have to keep a low profile as the 'bosses' of the project, and be paid discretely. As far as anyone knew, we were just part of the crew.

After a detailed survey of all the ragged edges, we came up with a list of things to challenge any good boat builder. She was an old girl, and was built in 1932 during the Depression when materials were dear and labor was super cheap. Everything we looked at had evidence of it, plus years of hard racing and general neglect had put her on the edge. There were troubles everywhere. Rot, leaks, blown bearings and gears, dead engines, and a host of other impending things we didn't know about until we ripped her open. We began to wonder if we had bitten off more than we could chew.

The crew was made up of 'volunteers' from the Opua/Russell area we had met during our stay there. Roberta gave Geoffrey the command of the crew and I would be the construction foreman. It didn't take her long to recruit a couple of other fellows from the local pubs she frequented every afternoon, and soon there were ten happy campers living in the various cubby holes on board, being fed and earning twenty NZD a week for the effort. And there was a promise of the glorious cruise when the job was done. Dreamers.

So we began. Roberta was all about the cosmetics. She wanted the beautiful teak rails stripped and oiled, and the bulwarks stripped and repainted. But as we did this, we found the well worn deck leaked and was only one and a quarter inches thick. This was probably done to save weight as well as money, but fifty years later it had been scrubbed a few too many times and now we were looking at reeving the seams and doing a black goo caulking job just to hold off the inevitable.

When we took every winch off its base and found all the broken pawls and worn bearings, we knew ordering spare parts was necessary. The huge windlass was removed and put on a truck to a recommended machine shop for a complete rebuild. Then the heavy chain could be handled more easily by a smaller crew. A diesel generator followed shortly after and the mechanic came and analyzed the rebuild of the main engine as well. New injectors and fuel filters would get it going again.

The main cabin top and doghouse had big blisters of paint from years of over-coating and when the crew started to strip it, we quickly found the covering material was totally rotten, probably the original as well. Sadly, the  cheap white pine planking under the canvas was also spongy and rotten. We were now opening a can of worms and they were crawling out everywhere. Once the planks went away, we then faced twenty rotten main cabin deck beams. This also was a ruse. Inside the cabin they looked to be Honduras mahogany. But it would not be so. In fact, they were more common red oak with thin veneers of mahogany covering the cheap wood, just another gift from the Depression. *Constellation* was turning out to be an old woman with layers of decaying makeup. We wanted to make proper laminated beams and remove the fake covering. Paint would make it fine. But Roberta would have none of it and demanded we keep the 'false paneling', as she called it. This was going to make the entire job more like a restoration than the rebuild for function it should have been, and certainly more work than we bargained. But we were in it now and the ball was rolling. We had ripped apart this old yacht and now were obliged to get her right again.

We knew the mast had some problems. We saw evidence of glue failure. A previous owner, who raced her hard, had placed two-inch wide stainless steel bands around it, every two feet, to keep the joints from spreading open. The decision was made to take the main mast out and do some repairs (the fore was solid still). Optimistic.

We moved 'Connie' alongside the yard space where a large crane came and lifted the mast out. It measured ninety feet in length and eighteen inches in diameter at the deck, tapering to six inches at the truck. When the crane picked it up with the hardware. it weighed nearly five thousand pounds.

All we could do was lay it on horses in the open yard and get to work. We planned on using a router to make grooves out of the glue joints that had opened up and then pump epoxy resin into the cracks, with strips of wood driven into the deep grooves to close it. Dreaming again.

The crew removed the metal bands. Three small bolts secured each band and as the bolts were removed we began to hear lots of cracking and creaking noises, as though some spirit was trying to escape after years of bondage. Then without much warning, the whole thing just started to fall apart. The fifty-year old glue was dust. Depending on location, some parts were huge timbers four inches thick and eight or ten inches wide. All the scarfs were upside down, so for years the seams leaked, and water ran down inside, rotting the entire core of the spar. We carefully labeled each piece that was solid enough to set in a pile and did a schematic drawing to show how the pieces reassembled. What was left was an odd core of pieces that was now more just a plank or two in the chain. It was still in one length, thankfully, but now we had a real piece of crap to deal with.

Geoffrey took over the mast project and Roberta conned the owner of a local lumber company and millworks to let us move the remains into his

shop to put it back together. But first we had to find wood for a job like this, a project in itself. Even though the wood came from sources all over the country, it would take weeks to find. Meanwhile we had plenty of other things to keep us busy. And the list seemed to be growing longer as more and more rot and decay continued to surface.

Now we had a fifty-year old boat with the cabin tops off, the main mast out, every mechanical part in pieces, and a window of time that was closing with the upcoming winter. All we could do now was keep the hammer falling and charge on. Plus, the *Seminole* was getting an equal amount of attention when the *Constellation* work was done for the day. She would get a new bottom, topsides painted, decks, mast, boom, interior refinished, a new propane stove, complete spinnaker gear, chain and anchors re-galvanized, and a hundred other tiny but necessary fixes. New Zealand was now only about work.

In the end we would get it all done. All the rebuilding, the painting, the main mast reconstruction and re-rigging, sail repairs and more reef points, the gear to make it all work, deck leaks repaired, main cabin and doghouse rebuilt, all winches back in place and up to the job, main engine rebuilt onboard, generator back functioning, windlass like new, and all with a crew of neophytes and dreamers. Sadly, the job we did to make the rig able to manage anything was more than the hull structure could handle. When Roberta and crew finally left New Zealand, they were able to sail her hard, which worked the stem loose, forcing them back to port. The fantasy voyage was over until a haulout and repairs could make her seaworthy again. In the end, almost none of the crew were able to get any reward for their efforts because the *Constellation* was stuck and most of them had to move on.

Geoffrey and I had completed our job and felt we could go without guilt. We loaded up the *Seminole*, put her in the water, and left town days later.

Dear Mom,

Two letters mailed on the same day! One was already sealed so I had to write another. *Seminole* is out of the water, on the hard, and there are a few things I will need before it can go back in the water.

First is a BJ Cutless bearing, a rubber bearing for the propeller shaft, 1 3/4" O.D. by 1 1/8" shaft diameter. I need one of these. Also, contact Peter if you can and find out from him what the parts number is for the inside working parts of a Dole thermostat for the Farymann diesel. A truck parts company should have it. I only need the inside. Try and find one around 180 F. If you can't find 180 F, get a 160 if you need to.

Also, we are desperate for weird music. Can't find any Miles Davis, Roland Kirk, Stanley Clark, Otis Redding, Pheobe Snow, or Joan Armatrading. Anything like that would be appreciated as this place is like 1951.

Constellation is a work barge now. We estimate seven weeks to complete the work we've begun. It's a forty-six year old wooden boat and every time we go to fix one thing, something else connected with it is rotten. The mast is now completely disassembled and the coach roof is slowly going back together. Plus there are a million loose ends, as the boat is nearly completely de-rigged as well. If we get it finished before our visas expire, we'll be real lucky. It's damn cold here now and I've had to dig out my red check wool jacket and moldy wool socks. It rains nearly every day and storms about once every ten days. A place fit only for ducks at this time of year. We are anxious to leave for sure.

Anything happen with the ad? Send the goods airmail... that should be fast enough, as *Seminole* will be out of the water for about three weeks from today. Send it to the Slipway address in Tauranga. Marianne and Geoff are turning out to be real friends and will be fine sailing mates, I'm sure. We've been talking with one of the young dairy farmers we met at Mayor Island and he may even go a ways with us. Port Villa in the New Hebrides should be the next stop. Thanks for your help. Buy the parts through Roger. I wrote him as well to ask for assistance.

Love,

Barry

SMOKED OYSTER SPAGHETTI
ALFA CENTAURI

When Geoffrey was bouncing around the Caribbean, he got a fantastic job onboard the *Alpha Centauri,* a Swan 65 belonging to the Berlusconi brothers; Sylvio being the famous one, now President of Italy. Part of Geoff's job was shopping and sharing the cooking, where he learned how to whip up the Berlusconi brothers' favorite dish out of simple stuff that was almost always handy on board.

SIMPLE VERSION

1 large can crushed peeled tomatoes
1 large onion
4 or 5 cloves garlic chopped
Crushed red peppers
Olive oil
2 cans oysters
Fresh basil
Mushrooms

Chop the onion in 1/2 in chunks and put in hot oil with red peppers. Stir around until clear; add mushrooms and oysters Then add the tomatoes, add garlic.

Add basil to taste and cook for 20 minutes. Let simmer.

Serve with cooked spagetti.

SMOKED OYSTER SPAGHETTI
ALFA CENTAURI

COMPLEX VERSION

4 large cans crushed peeled tomatoes
2 onions
5 cloves garlic chopped
1/2 cup fresh basil
1 large or 2 small fresh ripe cayenne peppers
1 can smoked oysters
1/2 lb tonbo (albacore, tuna, ono) cut in small cubes
6-8 large scallops, cut in small pieces
18 or so large shrimp
1 cup of mixed shitake and button mushrooms (would be chantrels)
Olive oil
No salt
No other spices
2 tbls red wine
1 tsp raw sugar

Chop the onion in 1/2 in chunks and put in hot oil with red peppers. Stir around until clear; add mushrooms and oysters Then add the tomatoes, add garlic.

Add basil to taste and cook for 20 minutes. Let simmer.

Add various seafood depending on cooking time. Tuna first, scallops, shrimp and cook a few more minutes.

Serve with cooked spagetti.

Dear Mom,

Today is May 12. Humpday. Kiwis are now coasting into the weekend and we are powering to try and get *Connie* water tight before the next winter gale hits. I finished covering the cabin top with plywood yesterday and am getting ready for the protective covering. I'm enclosing a news article about our thing here. I'm the mysterious Sticks Thompson. I've taken to using any name that comes to mind just for the hell of it. We got the mast into a covered space, so when it's raining we'll still get it finished. My visa expires June 6 and I really don't know if they'll let me stay, but Geoff and I are going to attempt to get the old girl sailing again. For days it seemed as though we'd never stop finding rot and decay, but now we are finally putting the thousands of pieces back together. Assuming we get the time and weather we need, we might be out of here in five or six weeks. The *Seminole* will be in top shape again with a new color scheme; dark green hull, pale yellow decks and cabin sides. Everything is repainted and repaired.

The bearing arrived today with no duty and is the right one. Many thanks for your trouble. As soon as I get thirty dollars, I'll send it to you. Also, Tom stopped by while I was working and said he'd left the package in Russell. It will have to wait until I sail back up there on the way out of NZ. Perhaps someone will even bring it down to me.

I expect to be in fair shape dollar-wise when I leave here. I hope to have enough to get to South Africa. When we leave here, we are going to the Hebrides, then Santa Cruz Island, New Guinea, Indonesia (probably Bali), Java, Sumatra and finally Sri Lanka. That is the next pit stop. Either stay there a full season, or head on to the Cape of Good Hope to make Carnival in Rio de Janeiro in February '79. There may be four of us now. A twenty-eight year old American woman I played with in Tahiti, named Iris, may join us. She knew Geoff from before and she and Lena get along well. No jealousy that is. Iris is from L.A., very independent, and good at sea. We all have mutual interest in "getting out of Dodge."

Did you every run the newspaper ad? Tell Harriett to write. I'd love to hear from her. Send news of Roger and Cath. I know they find it hard to write. I've written them. How about my father? I've written him as well.

I'm a little brought down hearing about Grandpa. I'm sure his pride and desire to not be pitied or made over will make him be able to pass away with all the dignity and grace he lived. The artificiality of hospital "life" is not fair to Grandma or the rest of the family and I hope none of you will be so selfish to try and keep him around in a half dead state for your own reasons. He's ninety-six years old, lived a full rich satisfying life and will not be loved less to be allowed to pass in peace. As much as I love him, I can't help but feel this way.

Love,

Sticks

GOOD CHOW

This is what you do when there's nothing going on.

8 whole cloves of garlic
Grind meat from 3 ripe coconuts
1 medium sweet potato
1 medium onion
1 tsp (or to taste) green Thai curry paste
2 tbls roasted sesame oil
1/2 cup fresh chopped basil
(you could use broccoli or zucchini)
Raisins, chopped peanuts, chopped shallots
1 cup sweet shredded coconut
Sliced cucumbers
Sweet mango chutney
1/2 cup of broth
Add chicken, pork, fish or meat to your Chow

Sauté onions, garlic and sweet potatoes in sesame oil. Cook until onions are clear and potatoes start to get soft. Add Thai curry paste and stir in. Keep sweet potatoes and onions brewing. Add some liquid to keep chow from sticking to side of pan.

Add 2 to 3 cups of roasted chicken or cooked pork, fish or meat and cook for another 5 to 8 minutes, constantly stirring. Squeeze coconut meat through cheese cloth to make cream. Put it into chow. Then add basil. Cook for another couple of minutes so it all blends in together.

Serve over brown rice with condiments – raisins, chopped peanuts, shallots, sliced cucumbers and sweet mango chutney.
Served with Sauvignon Blanc and Miles Davis.
Serves 4-6 people

Dear Mom,

I'm taking this piss-down rainy morning to let you know how things are going here in greater Tauranga. The tapes and parts arrived OK and are happily received. The part is the correct one. The '*Nole*' is getting back together finally. The bottom is sand-blasted and recoated and the topsides are painted a lovely dark green. The decks are all that remain. All we need is four or five days of good weather between now and the time we launch to get her going. I'm going to try and get a U.S. money order to send you, but it may be hard. They're really funny about money here. Lots of currency regulations. We hope to launch on June 16 and leave directly from Tauranga a few weeks later, direct to Port Villa in the New Hebrides. It's bitter cold here lately with south winds bringing freezing weather from the Antarctic. In the morning, it's always in the low 30's. Should've been gone long ago but the '*Connie*' kept us here. The mast is now re-laminated and only requires paint and re-rigging, the cabin top is nearly finished; all the finish work is nearly done. Only the loose ends remain.

I'm no longer working for Roberta as it's necessary to spend full time on my boat. Hard to believe I will probably leave NZ almost broke, as I've put nearly everything I've earned back into the boat. At least now she'll be in good shape for another year or so. And no matter what, I'll always have my skills to pull me through. I'd sure like to hear from Roger and Catherine about the cedar and spruce I asked about. Geoff has some money and would like to buy some wood to build a boat. If Roger is available it would be ideal, and Geoff is going to the States in August and could stop by and do the deal.

Believe it or not, I keep a tab on what I owe you for your favors, past and present, and value them as a sort of "loan". When the '*Nole*' sells, which she will some day, I intend to return what I must to keep myself straight. You just never know when the "buyer" will show up or how. The price is now forty-thousand dollars US as she is in superb shape inside and out. Ready to go the rest of the way around.

Since I won't be leaving here for around four weeks, people can still write me here at the slipway. Give my hellos to Paul and Sandy in S.D. and tell Paul I'll write him as soon as I get some time. I'm into an eight-day week for a while now so won't have much free time or energy. My hair is international travel short, like the old days, not at all like the enclosed photo, but that is still the way I feel. I guess I'll always like that "look" the best for me. But for ease of travel it's short, real short. I've got many friends here now, with comfortable old wooden houses and fireplaces. Lena (our new name for Marianne) and I often find ourselves in front of the fire at some friends house on a cold night.

Love to see you,

Barry

July 10, 1978
Tauranga

Dear Mom,

By tomorrow afternoon, July 10, we should be making our way north to Port Villa in the New Hebrides. Our work with *Constellation* is finished and the *Seminole* is as good as new. The hull is dark green, a red bottom and crème colored decks and cabins. She's stripped out and lighter than ever and moves easily with her new slick bottom. Every bit of hardware is renewed and we have a spinnaker for downwind.

God has been so good to me here, bringing me good fortune and the ability to keep going. Funny thing though, I can't get any dollars ahead. Tonight is the last night in town, and I know I'll be flat broke when we arrive in the next place. I don't write this to do more than let you know where I'm at. I earned and spent thirty-five hundred dollars here in NZ, ninety percent on the boat. She looks so beautiful, I don't care if I'm broke or not. The dance is to do now, not tomorrow. I can never wait to be happy or sad. I'm happy now with my friends, Geoff, Iris, and Lena. We all want this adventure.

I'm sad because of leaving so many more friends and lovers behind here in NZ. How many times I've left such fine friends behind. It can only be that many times I'll be made happy to see them again. I guess if you're a wanderer, you have to wander more quickly to keep in touch. I'm not going to write anyone else. There is so much delicious free time ahead. We should be at sea about ten days. Days growing warmer and longer as we go north. No more wool socks and rain. Empty pockets and warm hearts. No problems of money or papers, nothing. Out there it's just real things, without schedule or routine. The delicate dance on the waves suits me fine.

Since I won't know where I'll be on your birthday, I'll say Happiest Birthday to you now. I'm wearing those shirts, beaming from the compliments. Lena digs the pants so I wear them lots. I've cleaned up my act considerably with good clothes, short hair, and a together boat. Try it a different way for a while. Still the same inside though. Sometimes that's hard to hide if necessary. Oh well.

New address: c/o Port Captain, Port Villa, Efate Island, New Hebrides
My love to all. I'll write underway.

Love,

Barry

Last known photo of the Seminole
leaving Tauranga July 10, 1978

When you're naked and you've really got nothing,
you're not sitting there thinking about big things,
you're thinking about how you're going to get warm.

SHIPWRECK

Dear Mom

*Months of hard work to get Seminole in shape
for another couple of years of seagoing service
brought her to a state more finished than ever.
She was a tropic bird and we could feel
she was ready to go in every way.*

GO WITH WHAT YOU GOT

Three of us had been working for four months dedicated to the idea that in a few more weeks and after a thousand miles of ocean, we'd be back in the warm latitudes exploring our favorite islands. New Zealand was getting too damned cold for tropical birds and was becoming more miserable by the day. It was early July and we had already blown it by still being there so late in the season. No excuses. There was work to get done and we simply couldn't leave. Months of hard work to get *Seminole* in shape for another couple of years of seagoing service brought her to a state more finished than ever.

The hull was still beautifully fair, suffering no ill effects from the twenty thousand miles of ocean it had crossed, and it was now painted a rich dark green with a red boot stripe and creamy colored decks and cabins. She was as beautiful as any yacht in the yard. The Sitka Spruce spars had been in need of a fresh coat of paint, but otherwise were in perfect condition. Teak trim, rail caps and coamings were scrubbed to that wonderful silver gray that looks so ship shape and never stands out like boats which have varnish everywhere. *Seminole* was a tropic bird too and we could feel she was ready to go in every way.

Ebullience hardly describes the feeling when you know it's almost over and you're about to "get out of Dodge" again and be back on the open sea. Soon there would be no wool socks, sweaters, or drippy cold nights. We were only ten days away from the luscious latitudes and the relaxed island life. *THE* plan included a short pit stop in the New Hebrides to catch the end of the Tauranga to Port Villa yacht race, where we could make some money repairing Kiwi built sails blown out along the way, followed by a leisurely excursion through the Torres Straits to Indonesia.

Several days before our planned departure, the crew prepared a complete stores list in order to make the shopping easier during our final buying adventure in Auckland. Lena and I set out on a mission to the big city with a pocketful of cash and lists. When finished, we would be on our way.

It was the fourth of July and there had already been a couple of vicious storms. During one wild northeasterly gale we helped the crew of the *Constellation* keep her from bashing to bits against the mooring piles in the river. She was exposed to the full fetch of the wide harbor, and waves were

175

crashing hard against her port side and breaking over the deck. This was the full violence of a New Zealand winter storm and we weren't anxious to experience any more.

The cold rain of winter spotted the windshield of our battered car as we drove through the grayness across the Waikato valley to Auckland and two days of visiting chandleries and government bureaucrats. Luckily we were well organized and everything came together with little difficulty. Our last stop was an Oriental specialty shop. It was a place where you could get bulk food items such as beans, rice, and dried fruit. We had been there earlier in the summer and knew it was perfect for our needs.

Located in a run down part of town, the shop was in a rust red building sandwiched between two others which were boarded up and vacant. A small brass bell over the door rang as we entered.

I WOULD HAVE YOU GET DOWN ON YOUR HANDS AND KNEES AND I WOULD TAKE A BIG SWORD AND CUT OFF YOUR HEAD.

The musty smell of woven baskets, bamboo, grains, and incense took me away to another world. It was an Eastern oasis crammed with a fascinating array of weird stringed instruments, tapestries, and baskets. Carcasses of birds and fish, looking dried for years, hung from wooden dowels all along one wall.

As we entered we were approached by a young Chinese a foot and a half shorter than myself and slight of build. He appeared to be in his early twenties. In his crisp New Zealand accent he asked if he could help us. I whipped out my list and proceeded to rap out our needs in a very self assured manner. Lena and I were both surprised by his response.

"Excuse me, sir." he said calmly. "I think you have the wrong idea. Perhaps if you could go back outside and then come in and try again, it will be OK." I suppose it could have been my tone of voice or my abrupt Yankee style that had offended him.

"I didn't mean to offend you. We simply wish to buy some foods and be on our way."

Even his reply was unusual for a shopkeeper. He said, "We have a small friendly place here and are not used to doing this kind of business. Maybe you could go someplace else?"

All this greatly upset Lena. On the way there she told me that this young man was known to be a bit strange to his friends. His attitude bothered her and she wanted to leave immediately. I thought that was unnecessary and calmed her down. We selected what we wanted on our own, bagged it, and put it on the counter while he helped another customer. By his glances I could tell it was only a standoff of sorts. He eyed us as if we were going to steal something.

We moved to another corner of the shop to get some soy sauce. What was on display had been decanted into one liter wine bottles. I asked if it was possible to buy a single gallon or more in a plastic jug. Without a reply he looked at me, turned around, and walked into a rear area through a curtained doorway carrying the smaller bottles of the sauce.

When he returned he was empty handed. He walked straight to me, came very close and calmly said, "Do you know if I could have anything in the whole world right now, I would have you get down on your hands and knees and I would take a big sword and cut off your head."

I couldn't believe what I was hearing. Reacting to what I took for a joke I laughed aloud. From his reaction I could tell it wasn't meant to be funny.

"Why do you laugh?" he replied grimly.

"I don't think it's particularly funny. It's just I've never had anyone say anything like that to me. It's ludicrous. I came here to buy food, not to have trouble. If it's a problem, then we'll pay for what we've already selected and we won't bother you any more." Lena was now trying to get me to leave without taking anything with us, but I wasn't as bothered by him as she was and it seemed to be no problem to me.

There was now an uncomfortable truce between us while we completed the transaction, minus the soy sauce. He became strangely calm, continuing to insist my attitude was completely wrong, that I showed no respect, and I should make amends. When our business was finished we left without lingering. The jingle of the bell on his door echoed in my thoughts as we drove away.

I was trying to leave him there in his little store but it seemed as though his fruits, nuts, and grains filled the car with his angry presence. Having no more to do in Auckland, we headed out of town and into the rich green dairy region of the Waikato Valley. The sky was full of dark clouds and rain fell intermittently. Several times during the long trip back to the *Seminole* the image of the young Chinese fellow's face was clear in my mind, making me think about the strange incident earlier in the day.

It was nearly dark when we returned to the slipway. *Seminole* glowed under the yard lights like a brand new boat. She was ready to get off the hard. We had been sitting for the last four months and needed to be at sea. What a relief it would be to float again! We lived aboard the whole time we were hauled and working on the boat. Painting and varnishing the interior and cooking and eating and sleeping down below in the bad weather made for a constant mess. It was the pits. We were ready to rock and roll.

The plan was to load all the stores and clean the boat while it was still high and dry. Then we would launch and leave the next day for Port Villa. Besides the ever present threat of nasty winter storms urging us to leave, there was the fact that our visas were expired, even after several extensions. And the Bureaucracy doesn't give a damn about the weather.

The next morning the crane had us in the water without a hitch, hardly scratching the new paint. She was brand new, better than I had seen

AN IMAGE OF THE CHINESE FELLOW WAS AS CLEAR IN MY THOUGHTS AS THE VISION OF THE ORANGE FIREBALL.

her in almost ten years. We powered over to the *Gypsy Rose*, a friend's eighty foot tuna clipper, put out fenders and tied alongside to have a shower and farewell dinner in their spacious galley. The skipper turned on his newfangled weatherfax machine and got the latest map for the area. All the isobars were far apart without a low in sight. It looked as though our departure day would be sunny and fine. Our confidence was high.

We were to meet customs and immigration at the town docks in the morning. The *Seminole's* crew had made so many new friends while in Tauranga and a troop of them showed up to wish us Bon Voyage. It's always hard to leave a good place behind and the farewells were mixed with admonitions to return.

July 10, 1978 was a perfectly fine morning with clear skies and puffy cumulus clouds that reminded us of the Trades. The weatherfax for the morning was still all clear giving us no reason to hang on for another minute. Before we were a half mile down the river, *Seminole* was sliding along under full main and genoa charging for the open sea. We waved to all our friends who had driven to the point for their last look and it was goodbye Kiwi land.

That day's sailing was uneventful and mild, so mellow that no one was feeling seasick even after four months of land locked life. We had the new spinnaker flying as we headed offshore into an obviously dying breeze, the sky still full of fluffy balls of clouds, very uncharacteristic of thirty eight degrees South latitude, especially in winter.

Shortly before sunset we were down to a crawl, the breeze at about five knots. All four of us were sitting in the cockpit having a rum when a tremendous orange ball of flame lit the twilight sky. It appeared to come from just above the Eastern horizon and grew in size as though it were coming right at us. For a moment it was gigantic and then it sank slowly into the sea. All of us watched the entire phenomenon amazed.

The others chattered excitedly about what they had just seen, while I sat quietly. An image of the Chinese fellow was as clear in my thoughts as the vision of the orange fireball.

Night fell on a glassy sea so calm the stars reflected like bits of broken glass. During the mild night watches we made slow progress to the North and by dawn we could no longer see Mayor Island. The sky became gray with occasional drizzle and there was a light but building breeze. The big blue number one was full and drawing and it wasn't long before the leeward rail was awash most of the time. One by one we passed the numerous small islands that surround the tip of the Coramandel Peninsula, keeping in mind to maintain a healthy amount of sea room. A swell was building along with the breeze and *Seminole* was coming alive, but unfortunately so were the crew's stomachs.

I felt queasy and tired but under control. The others suffered more, with Geoffrey spending a good amount of time over the lifeline calling O'Rourke. Lena and Iris fared better. None of this went well with the continually deteriorating conditions. As we had our afternoon get together in the cockpit we were in full winter foul weather gear, wet, cold, and feeling a bit sluggish and lazy. Dripping rain and spray was ruining our cocktail hour. Great Barrier Island was visible in the haze about twelve to fifteen miles to leeward, and there was discussion about seeking shelter near Blind Bay to avoid a night of slogging through the cold rain. We all agreed it was too close to dark to attempt entering a strange anchorage. Instead we set a course that would take us well clear and we were looking forward to the safety of the open sea. Our bodies and minds were tired and ready to rest.

As the moonless blackness settled over us, the seas were becoming quite confused. There was not a star, cloud cover was total, and the rain made it hard to see the bow from the cockpit. Where was this fine weather the map had showed us? Lena and I took the eight to midnight watch leaving Iris and Geoffrey to sleep. A small headsail and two reefs in the main kept us slogging along. I went below about 11:30 and woke Iris so she could get into her foul weather gear and help us get the main down. Geoffrey had taken refuge on the cabin sole and was resting so I decided to let him be. After all we were only going to tack offshore and heave-to anyway. There was no reason to wake him. He needed the rest break from the incessant puking. Iris said she didn't mind being on watch alone. She joined us around twelve and we dropped and lashed the main and put the helm over. The boat was now lying quietly making a knot or two on a course offshore.

At the change of the watch the conditions were ugly. Continuous torrential rain and forty knot winds with higher gusts limited visibility to the range of our diving light. It was a light sword piercing the blackness, a brilliant hole in the night full of sparkling raindrops. The boat was on an offshore heading with the wind veering from the Northeast to the North. We were relatively comfortable but taking an occasional green one over the deck. When I felt sure that Iris was all right, I went below, stripped naked and slipped into a clean dry bunk already warm with Lena's heat. What a nice feeling after hours of sitting in the cold and rain! I fell quickly into a dreamy sleep.

Iris is the kind of crew you like to have on board. She was strong, tough, and had easily as many sailing miles as me on a variety of boats. She worked her way on deck throughout the South Pacific. Iris knew the *Seminole* quite well. She'd sailed on her many times before, had good dry foul weather gear and boots, and seemed comfortable with her solitary watch.

But still it happened. In retrospect there were many things that could have been done but these are only lessons learned. Mistakes I hope I never **ROCKS! BARRY, WE'RE ON THE ROCKS!** make again. It was a terrifying moment when everything in our lives became agonizingly different as we were jarred from our sleep by Iris' gut wrenching scream. "Rocks! Barry, we're on the rocks!!"

Almost at the same moment Lena and I were hurled from the pilot berth to the cabin sole. The boat groaned and crashed with a horrible lurch. What a way to wake out of peaceful dreams! Before I could get on deck, *Seminole* hit again with the same awful grinding sound. No time for clothes.

Geoffrey was still in his full foul weather gear, having fallen asleep with them on. Lena was naked and it was so bloody cold. The air temperature was probably in the high forties with the water only a few degrees higher. Bouncing from one side of the cabin to the other with each smash on the rocks I made my way up to the cockpit and hit the starter and heard the faithful little two cylinder come to life. By this time the *Seminole* had crashed heavily several times. There was no time to grieve, only act.

I grabbed the wheel and it spun freely. The tiller had broken at the rudderhead.

Masthead and running lights dimly lit what appeared to be a sheer cliff along our port side. To starboard was group of rocks, barely submerged. We were trapped between the cliff and these rocks. Iris manned the throttle and I leaped over the stern, figuring to be able to stand on the brace for the self steering vane. When I was ready to steer I screamed through the gale and the crunching sounds for Iris to hit the throttle. With the prop churning water just inches from my feet we pulled away from the rocks every time the hull rode up on the surge.

The others were screaming we had made it. We had. We were clear of the terrible jaws of the rocks. But what now? There was only the stormy blackness. No safety in sight.

Our elation was short lived. The little motor choked and died leaving us silently adrift again in the raging storm. We made about five hundred yards from the place where we hit but would soon blow back against the cliff at the rate we were going.

WE WERE CLEAR OF THE TERRIBLE JAWS OF THE ROCKS. BUT WHAT NOW? THERE WAS ONLY THE STORMY BLACKNESS. NO SAFETY IN SIGHT.

Lose one battle, fight another. The next step was to stop her from drifting back into the rocks. All our ground tackle was lashed in chocks for the passage but with a sharp knife and quick fingers I quickly had the 45 lb. CQR anchor and chain over the side. There was a powerful tug as the anchor set itself with about two hundred feet of scope. Another small victory but no time for any celebration. Where were the others? What was happening back aft?

Heart pounding, mind reeling, adrenaline pumping, my every sense alive. There was no knowing what the others were doing. *Seminole* was sluggish and dead in the water.

Geoffrey thought we needed an anchor that was stowed in the engine room under the cockpit. There was little more than a crawl space under the lift-up companionway ladder into the small area that housed the tanks, batteries and motor. When he got inside there were streams of water six inches in diameter coming through several holes punched right around the waterline. The engine room lights were still on when he entered but as the water hit the tops of the batteries, the light turned to pitch black. One can only imagine his terror in the rapidly filling blackness as he groped his way back into the main cabin wondering if he would get out before she went down.

The icy water was nearly to the top of the engine room door when he escaped into the main cabin. There he found Iris looking for her backpack, which she knew contained a Swiss army knife, tobacco and matches and her documents. He told her to get out immediately as the water was already hip deep and not slowing down.

Lena was in the cockpit working the bilge pump with all her heart, as if believing she could pump the hull dry with enough effort. What a way to begin her seagoing adventures. Iris came on deck with life jackets, one

SHE WAS UNDERWATER LOOKING UP THROUGH THE BUBBLES WHILE THE MAST AND RIG SLID DOWN ON HER.

for each of them. She grabbed the high powered diving light. Meanwhile Geoffrey had gone aft to free the survival valise from the stern cabin coachroof.

All this took place in a matter of a minute or two. This boat was sinking fast. I tore at the lashings on our nine foot inflatable and got the wad of it loose in my arms. I was just opening the first of the CO2 bottles when the stern went awash. I yelled that everyone should get off and away from the boat, jumped into the icy sea, and lost my grip on the partially inflated dinghy. I swam a few strokes to get clear and turned to see what was happening.

Sputtering and thinking I had really blown it this time, that this just might be the end, I turned back to see what was to become of my beloved home of six years. The last view of *Seminole* was the forward ten or twelve feet of her, bowsprit pointing toward the sky. Then she slipped quickly below the surface, exhaling a final breath out the forward ventilator. She was gone.

Whoa! Was it cold! Keep moving. Keep breathing. One minute a dreamy warm sleep, the very next a fight for life. There was the Chinese guy again.

fore than an image...a clear picture of his small face, bright in my mind. No time for that, what about the others?

Geoffrey had no time to even cut the lashings on the sack of gear we had prepared for emergency. The boat sank so fast he had to jump off the port side along with me and was clear and safe. But the two women were on the other side of the boat when she started to go down. Iris made it clear away but Lena was still in the cockpit. Afraid to move and trapped beneath the canvas dodger, she was sucked below the surface as the boat sank stern first. She later told us how she was underwater looking up through the bubbles while the mast and rig slid down on her. She said she felt the boat was her security and just couldn't bring herself to jump over the side. When it slid away so quickly there was no chance to get clear. Probably thirty five feet down, she looked to the surface and all around her was aglow as if all the lights in the world were on, a million brilliant bubbles rising into a white glow. But there were no more batteries, no lights, no moon, only the blackness. She saw the light.

Clawing through the wires and tangle of halyards and rigging, she made it to the surface and found herself near Iris who was flashing the diving light. By then Geoffrey and I were near each other trying to scream through the wind to maintain contact in the raging blackness. We could hear other yelling and saw the light flashing occasionally but we didn't know if they were both there.

The water was so cold it quickly numbed my nakedness. I knew that getting out fast was imperative. Hypothermia would kill us quickly. We could see the light flash along the cliffs. As far as we could make out there was only sheer rock walls coming straight up out of the sea.

THE WATER WAS SO COLD IT QUICKLY NUMBED MY NAKEDNESS. Geoffrey and I stayed as close together as we could manage, screaming loudly as we could to maintain contact in the dark. It had been about ten minutes since the boat was gone. It was some relief to hear both of the women scream back and know they were with us. We kept swimming toward the cliffs. The closer we got the more dangerous it became as a large swell smashed on the jumbled rocks at the base of the cliffs. The light would flash at a spot, then

Geoff and I would swim in until we could feel the swell begin to pitch. If all there was in front of the wave was a black hole full of jagged rubble, we'd back off to a safe distance and work our way farther along the cliff face, still screaming to keep in touch.

Finally there was an outcropping that looked as if it offered some safety from the breakers. We thought it looked like it could be approached without us getting too shattered. I went close first and a wave picked me up and dumped me rudely on some sharp lava. The stuff was like knives, a giant pumice from bubbling molten rock that had hit the sea. When the bubbles burst and cooled they had created a razor sharp surface. Fortunately the wave threw me quite high up and fairly gently at that. Scrambling like a crab I found a secure hold just out of reach of the next wave and received only a few choice cuts to show for it.

HOW LONG WOULD THE COLD NIGHT HAVE BEEN IF ONE OF US HADN'T MADE IT?

Geoffrey didn't fare as well. He missed the ride to the top and instead was sucked over the falls into the backwash alongside my precarious perch. He disappeared in the foamy whiteness and then popped up outside the breaker line a lifetime later. The next good sized wave then swept him onto the base of my little ledge, and he too scrambled out of the grip of the sea, badly cut and bleeding.

We both then yelled until we were coughing with hoarseness. We must have been heard because soon the light was trained on our spot. It wasn't too long until Lena and Iris did the crab trick too. With some help getting out of the water, they were safe as well. Sitting on the ragged lava huddled tightly together for warmth and comfort we talked sparingly about what our next move might be.

I took the light and tried to find a way up and out. Behind us was a sheer wall of rock straight up about four hundred feet. There appeared to be nothing but cliffs on either side of our little ledge as far as we could see. By this time it was about one A.M. We had been in the water around twenty minutes.

Five hours till dawn. Then what? We had no idea where we were, even what land. None of this made any sense. There wasn't supposed to be an island here. We were flashing an SOS about every fifteen minutes, but I don't think anyone was watching.

We all sat quietly and reflected on our survival. At least we were four. How long would the cold night have been if one of us hadn't made it? It would have been an agonizing chill far worse than anything physical we were suffering from being wet and naked in the night.

After I calmed down a bit from the exertion and the adrenaline level subsided, there was a terrifying feeling of the presence of the young Chinese again. So much that I spoke of it to the others. They must have thought I was mad. Here we were wiped out, lucky to be alive, and I was raving about this little guy as though he might have had something to do with it! Humor him, he's had a rough night.

After awhile none of us were talking much at all. We were only interested in conserving energy and body heat. We jammed together sharing our warmth and clothes. Geoffrey had ditched his foul weather gear pants and boots in the interest of swimming. He gave me a heavy sweater. Neither of us had pants. Lena had a foul weather gear top and Iris was still in her full length "banana suit" and had saved her boots. We sat on the two life jackets. I don't think any of us moved in our little huddle for four hours.

CHATTERING FROM HYPOTHERMIA AND MILD SHOCK AS WELL, WE HAD NO CHOICE BUT TO GET DOWN INTO THE WATER AND MOVE ALONG THE BASE OF THE CLIFF, A JAGGED SHEER FACE WITH NO TRAIL OR FOOTHOLDS.

With the coming of light we could see we were trapped at the base of a vertical cliff. Six or eight miles in the distance loomed another large land mass. There was no telling how large ours was. It was getting colder all the time as the wind was nearly Southwest by now, blowing straight out of Antartica, much colder than when it was Northeast.

We knew it wasn't wise for us to waste a single bit of the body heat and energy we had left. Now that we could see, we had to move. Chattering from hypothermia and in mild shock as well, we had no choice but to get down into the water and move along the base of the cliff, a jagged sheer face with no trail or footholds.

Partly crawling on big rocks and partly swimming, we made our way in the water several hundred meters to the North where we found the entrance to a large cave at about the tide level. It was deep and dark but offered a degree of shelter from the biting cold wind. Groping along until our eyes adjusted to the low light, we crawled off the jumble of rocks just inside the entrance onto sand that had been driven inside by countless storms. It was actually almost dry at the point where a tangle of driftwood seemed to bar our way.

By this time we were talking of how great it would be if some of this wood at the back of the pile might be dry enough to rub into a fire. There was a book of matches in Iris' bag which might have dried if there was sunshine. We didn't waste too much time on that because the deeper we got into the cave and over the pile of wood, the more it seemed like there was light further along. As if passing through to new life we pressed on, scrambling over the logs to eventually find the cave twisted through the cliff and opened into a shallow bay.

The floor of the other entrance to the cave was all large round rocks covered with oysters and mussels. At the opening, a steady trickle of sweet, fresh water seeped out of the rock walls. We smashed and ate the raw shellfish and drank our fill of the precious liquid. There were also other prizes in the little bay as odd bits of fruit and vegetables from the *Seminole* could be seen floating among the rocks on the other side of the cove. Getting warm was more of a priority than a few apples and cabbages though. It was decided to attempt to climb the cliff, which at this point didn't seem as imposing as it had on the other side of the cave.

The first forty feet or so was the most hazardous but by helping each other and moving cautiously, a level was reached where we could tell animals had been there. Then it became more like a difficult hike to the grassy top of the cliff where we were greeted with the full blast of the freezing and freshening Southwest wind.

I was the first to see where we were. It was a scene from some fairy tale, almost too cute to be real. The island that changed our lives was just a

dot in the ocean which we could now see from shore to shore. There was green grass on the slopes of a bowl shaped valley, trees scattered near the ridges, and all dotted with black lava rocks and a mixture of cattle and sheep. U-Shaped and open to the Northeast, it was cut down to the bottom by a little stream which ran into the bay. The mouth of the horseshoe was quite narrow and had a cliff at each side. The protected inlet was ringed with a white sand beach where stood a rough corral and a small shed. About two hundred meters up the stream bed a small house with smoke coming out of the chimney made our relief complete. With white clouds racing in the gray skies above us we laughed at how lucky we were now that it seemed we wouldn't simply freeze to death waiting for some matches to dry out.

Within minutes of reaching the cliff top we could see a burly man and his two dogs running up the hill towards us. The dogs were barking wildly and he was bounding like a mountain goat. We must have been quite a sight, three of us naked from the waist down and the fourth in her yellow suit standing on the ridge top as if deposited from the sky.

"Clive Abbot's the name." he said, "My dogs only bark when there's people around, so I knew something was up. How did you get here?"

The story spilled out of us chattering and shivering as we stumbled our way down the hill to the little house. Clive told us he and his wife, Sarah, lived alone on this dot of land which he called Arrid Island. They served as caretakers for the cattle and sheep that grazed in the rich green pasture and had been there for about six years.

He moved gracefully over the slippery, rocky terrain and wore no shoes, even though it was icy cold. I was barefoot too and was so cold I could only wonder why he would purposefully go outside without shoes if he had any to wear.

As we approached the house we could see it was only little more than a shack with a generator shed on one side and a small porch for hanging clothes and removing your shoes. He hustled us in the house and introduced us to Sarah. She seemed much older than he, all pinched, frail, and gray and didn't waste much time letting us know we might be intruding on their very private existence. Never the less they quickly went about building a fire under the water heater and put the kettle on the stove for tea. One by one we were sent into the bath, and the steaming water running over us soon had warmth returning to our extremities. A loan of fluffy dry clothes completed our rescue.

Sarah made us white bread toast and tea and served it on delicate plates at the small bare table in the tiny kitchen. It was probably the most people she ever had in her house at one time. And what a group it was!

Now dressed in Clive and Sarah's clothes a bit of who we were was hidden from their sight. But if it had mattered to them they might have seen that fate had dumped some unusual folks on their doorstep, and they had taken them in. There was no way they could have known of the trials that waited for us all in the future. Perhaps if they knew, they would have thought twice about helping us. But for the moment there was nothing but human kindness and caring. Chances were Clive and Sarah had little in common with us, except we were now wearing their clothes and had a mutual need for food and shelter.

After we finished eating and had a brief telling of our tale, Clive hustled us off to bed to get some rest and further warm our frozen bodies. Outside, the storm was blowing itself out from the Southwest, occasionally clearing and bringing much lower temperatures. The Abbots put Lena and I into their room, while Geoffrey and Iris went to the bunk beds in the tiny space next to the bath. That was the extent of the house; two small bedrooms, the bathroom, and a kitchen/parlor combination.

I snuggled into the wonderfully soft clean sheets made up perfectly on the old iron framed bed. Lena pressed against my body just as she had only a few hours before, and we quickly drifted off to sleep. It was about 8:30 in the morning.

It was a dream world in a soft bed with a down comforter and lace pillowcases. The room was pale yellow with almost nothing in it. The one window was made of a dozen small panes and framed the green image of rugged pasture land. Waking next to the warm softness I thought 'I'm still in the dream.' Bright afternoon sunlight sparkled on us through the facets of the curtain-less window. Why are we here? Is this a fantasy?

No. We were alive and every breath was elation! Lying in that wonderful bed and simply breathing was like floating on a cloud. The whiteness, the sunlight, the comfort and security, were heaven on Earth. We were alive and for those fragile moments it was as much as I could bear.

But there was a feeling of dread that was the memory of the little Chinese man. Lena lay serenely sleeping beside me as I scanned the room with my eyes absorbing every wonderful detail. I could feel it again. My mind was just beginning to accept the truth of this new reality when I felt him to be there too. I began to ask myself the first of a thousand questions I would not have answers for without seeing him face to face again.

HE SAID THERE WAS NO SIGHT OF ANY OTHER WRECKAGE, ONLY THE FLOATING BITS OF FRUIT AND VEGETABLES. THE SEMINOLE HAD SIMPLY DISAPPEARED BENEATH THE SEA.

A few hours later I got up and dressed in Clive's clothes. The pants came only a little below my knees and the plaid wool shirt could barely be tucked in them. The sleeves were about six inches too short. But it wasn't a fashion show. This would be it until we could put something else together.

Geoffrey was already up. He and Clive were talking and trying to make something out of our situation. The essence was that we were going to be here for sometime and we had no choice. Clive told us the place was called Arrid Island and belonged to the Brice family in Auckland. It was two hundred twenty acres, located about three miles East of Great Barrier Island and was the home of a hundred or so sheep, forty head of beef cattle, and one milk cow. There was a woolshed and a small winter barn a few hundred meters down the hill. The corral was for loading and unloading the barge boat that visited usually once every two or three months, bringing supplies and taking away the fattened animals. An ancient diesel generator out behind the small house provided power to chill the freezer once a day, run the electric lights and TV for the news and a program or two, and charged the batteries for the twice daily communication network. The ham radio was their only link with the outside world.

The nearest population of any consequence is in two small villages on Great Barrier Island, one around the corner in the North and the other in the South. Any radio contact with the mainland of New Zealand had to go through a third party in one of those two towns because Clive's radio could only reach that far. Other than the odd fishing boat, no one was listening for transmissions except during two scheduled fifteen minute periods, morning and afternoon.

To further increase the isolation, the same storm that wrecked the *Seminole* had bashed Clive's thirty foot launch on the rocks at the head of the little bay below the house. They were as marooned as we were. Clive's concern showed as he also told us the barge that normally brought their supplies had missed a trip last month due to foul weather and wasn't due for another three weeks. They had enough for the two of them if they were careful, but now with four new mouths to feed they would be cleaned out in a few days. He figured it would blow strong and cold from the Southwest for a couple more days, and after it moderated we might be able to get some help.

By the time the afternoon radio connection rolled around we had a fair assessment of our situation. Plainly we were shipwrecked on Arrid Island until further notice. I don't know how the others felt but I know for myself it was quite fine just to be breathing. I was high as a kite!

Our first goal was to let Lena's family know what had happened and we were safe and sound. We also contacted the *Gypsy Rose* and began the game of trying to get off the island. It didn't take long to realize having everything digested and retransmitted by a third party was going to make communication extremely complicated and unreliable. With darkness upon us so early and exhausted as we were, we could manage little but a light meal before heading to bed. All four of us were now sleeping in the tiny extra room. There was about a foot between the single size cot Lena and I shared and the single bunk beds for Geoffrey and Iris.

Clive and Sarah's routine was well established and it didn't take brain surgery to get the idea she wanted no part of anything new. She was awake and moving around at least an hour before dawn, probably doing the same little chores every day, feeding dogs and cats, milking the cow, and making tea. I woke up from the noises and stared into the chilly darkness, still a little surprised to not be in my bunk on board the *Seminole*. That feeling went away quickly while I replayed the last moments in the gale. What had gone wrong? What difference did it make now?

We were all up early for more tea and toast and to hear the morning network. So far there was no word from the mainland. Our radio connection, Fred, had little to offer. The sky had turned more gray and cold again and there was nothing to do but sit and wait.

The shock of the shipwreck and our landing was wearing off so we didn't feel as though we were in outer space anymore. But the chill was bone deep. Even with warmth and sleep I still felt cold clear through. Whenever I'd get outside my teeth would chatter and my body would shiver uncontrollably. It would be days before this was not the case, and to this day, whenever I get cold and begin to think of how it was then, I cannot keep from feeling this way.

Clive disappeared for a few hours and returned with a sack full of apples, oranges, cabbages, tomatoes, and other bits of stuff that had floated into the little bay we found after going through the cave. Geoffrey watched him and told us later Clive carried a small dinghy weighing over a hundred pounds up the hill behind the house and down the same cliff we had struggled to scale. He rowed around in the little bay picking up the goodies, then carried the dinghy and the full bag of stuff back up the cliff and down to the house. This guy was a powerhouse.

He said there was no sight of any other wreckage, only floating bits of fruit and vegetables. The *Seminole* had simply disappeared beneath the sea.

That afternoon we all went out to bring in firewood and help move the cattle onto another part of the island. It was incredibly rugged and aside from a small patch of trees, was almost completely grass and rock. Oh yes, and lots of cold, wet, mud. For some reason I always got the pair of gumboots with the holes. It never bothered Clive though because he never wore any shoes!

The weather deteriorated further and the shelter of the little house was the only place to be as the winter's darkness settled on our bleak new home. There was another session on the radio and a conversation with the Constable on Great Barrier to assure him that we were all unhurt and in good health. Getting into our new routine, we made a meal of what was left in the Abbot's larder and the gifts from the *Seminole*. We watched the news and then turned lights out, generator off, and went to bed.

The four of us in the tiny room with the bunk beds and the early bedtime simply got us into another space. By now we were well rested and just getting wound up at bedtime. It was too early for kids like us to hit the hay, so we lay in the dark and talked, probably much too much. Sarah burst in, making a sshh sound and told us to quiet down.

The third morning after breakfast, Geoffrey and I were talking about our Chinese nemisis and all the possibilities of guru/student or arch rival relations. Everyone in the house was tolerant, but Clive and Sarah were reacting with surprise that I was laying out all these strange scenarios. Was he an evil force to be defended against? Perhaps I should attack

FROM DEEP IN MY GUTS I CONJURED UP A HORRENDOUS SCREAM, A PRIMAL HOWL OF ANGUISH, A CURSE AT WHATEVER FORCES HAD PUT ME WHERE I WAS.

him? Maybe he was my teacher of all teachers? Should I go to him and whack his head off before he does any more harm? Should I bring him a sword and put my life in his hands? Was it possible that a curse or the power of his will could bring us such misfortune? It was a rambling, confused dialog with a tolerant friend who probably thought I was going crazy.

But I knew I wasn't crazy. Stranger things had happened to people and I had read of many of them. I was prepared for anything to be true. My whole life had changed in an instant and would probably never be the same. Gone were the carefree days of detached wandering on my comfortable yacht. Now there was only precious life! Elation mixed with the thought of everything being new. All physical connections with the past were washed away. Only the fresh brightness of the day was waiting.

Suddenly in the midst of our discussion I just had to get out of the house and away from the crowded, small room. With a polite excuse I stood and walked outside, grabbing a jacket on the way out the door. No one seemed to pay much attention except the dogs. They were happy to run along, the wind and cold never a bother to them.

Trudging up the grassy slope, I slipped in the mud. The image of Clive carrying the dinghy up that same hill made me laugh as I huffed along nearly out of breath before reaching the crest of the hill. And I was carrying nothing but my thirty two year old body. Precious breath. That was the end of cigarettes for me.

At the top of the hill I was on the same spot where we stood as we first surveyed the island. All along the ridge the grass stopped at a ragged shear line that fell straight away to become the cliffs we smashed against. Hundreds of feet below, the gray green sea washed on the black rocks, gently covering them with white foam. The icy Southwest wind tore at my face and hands as I struggled to stand at the edge of the cliff, leaning out to get a look at the open bay below.

From deep in my guts I conjured up an horrendous scream, a primal howl of anguish, a curse at whatever forces had put me where I was. On and on, seeking relief from the loss I felt, my voice was an instrument of my pain.

But I couldn't sustain it. The grayness opened here and there to patches of blue sky where the clouds were soft white. No matter which direction I looked there was awesome beauty and nature's power. Sunlight stabbed through a mist of rain and the resultant rainbow replaced my anguish with joy. I could no longer scream. My next breath turned into the sound of happy laughter mixed with tears as I let go of the resentment of cruel fate and accepted the gift of my life.

It came as quite a shock then to be suddenly tackled at the waist and wrestled back from the precipice by Clive. We rolled down the hill together like a log, coming to rest in the wet grass, his arms still tightly locked around me. I didn't comprehend this at first and could only manage to lie in his arms, laughing and crying like a fool.

"We could hear you screaming all the way down at the house. I thought you had lost yourself and were going to do something crazy, like jump off the cliff." He puffed from the exertion of running up the hill.

I had to chuckle. "Yes Clive, I admit the thought did cross my mind, but I've gone through too much in surviving to waste it all killing myself. I needed to come up here and get it out of my system. These rainbows and green islands are too wonderful to leave behind. But thanks anyway for caring about me. You are so very good to us." Then he quietly held me and let me cry until Lena came and touched me too. What I had lost suddenly became less important during those few precious moments.

Eventually we stood on the ridge saying nothing, just looking at that earthly scene. In the distance, clouds hung in the valleys of Great Barrier Island, dark green in its winter cover. Colors vibrated with the energy of the cold gale winds. Trees at the Southern crest of the little island stood firm above the emerald pastures while brown cattle and gray sheep grazed peacefully oblivious to any of our trivial tragedies. Nothing could have been more perfect.

Clive burst out excitedly, "Look, don't you see it? There. About a quarter mile out. It's your boat. I can see the deck and the mast under the water!"

The sea was blue where the sky had cleared above it and the sun cast its light from over our shoulders. It was true. The outline of the light colored decks and the white spars showed up sharply through the bright blue water. I stared for awhile, aware that Clive was much more excited than me. When the *Seminole* was totally gone, there was no need for decisions or obligations to that part of my past. Suddenly life was very complicated again.

Clive slipped away leaving Lena and I to walk back to the house alone. Silently, hand in hand, we made our way to the beach far away from the house and found a spot of sunshine between two huge rocks. The sand was dry and the wind couldn't find us in there. Small purple flowers grew from the cracks in the stone. Neither of us had much to say. We just quietly sat and she held me while I cried again.

That evening our discussions turned to the next plan of action. "The crew" was enthusiastic and supported the idea of some type of salvage. Now that we knew the boat was in fairly shallow water it was possible to at least save the gear, tools, and personal effects on board by diving with SCUBA. Once we knew what the state of her was, we could make some decision about any other salvage work. Iris was an experienced diver and was anxious to help with anything that could be arranged. Geoffrey pledged his personal cash to the effort, and it left me to decide whether to walk away or start a new life without digging up the old.

Clive said he knew of a fellow who had a boat and the dive gear and thought we could make some arrangement by radio. The wave of enthusiasm and optimism swept me into a decision. Before we knew it he had the guy on the radio, the Captain of the *Cleo*, a forty foot fishing boat. He had been monitoring our other transmissions and already knew quite a bit about our situation. Fortunately Clive had always been careful to never say on the air exactly where the *Seminole* had gone down. He said if he did, the place would soon be crawling with scavengers making good on our misfortune.

We were to give the Captain the night to see if he could find crew, sufficient gear, and supplies. If he could get it together we would talk again in the morning to strike some agreement on fees and costs. My mind reeled at the thought of committing to spend money I didn't have to save things which now meant little to me, and would never pay the bills, but Geoffrey's assurance gave me the confidence to say it was all right.

Clive arranged with the Brices to have food brought in by plane the next day. He had butchered a sheep on the fourth day, and we were eating that for dinner, with apples and cabbage from the wreck. None of the four of us minded at all, considering the alternative we would have faced had the Abbots not been there.

The strain of all the extra people appeared to be showing on Sarah. She looked ten years older than Clive and in fragile health. She told Lena she had a serious heart condition and had a heart attack before they moved out there. He was very good to her and did all but the light work around the house. They had chosen to be on the island because they loved the quiet and didn't like life around the city anymore. The years out there had been good to them and Sarah's heart could handle the gentle pace of the peaceful island.

But now what? Iris and Lena were dressed in her spare clothes looking all young and attractive, always joking and playing with "Zee Bull" as they called Clive. They went walking and exploring the island with him, while he went about his work with the livestock. Iris had her tobacco, saved from her backpack, carefully dried and rolled in newsprint. Sarah just couldn't quite handle it, and after only those few days the tension was building.

Clive seemed to like it all. He thrived on work and action. The adventure of possibly raising the wreck, hauling the dinghy, or having to kill a sheep so we could eat, seemed to make him more powerful and alive than he had been before. So much new youthful energy shattered his normally relaxed routine and brightened his eyes. Especially his eyes on the ladies.

In the morning, Clive had the captain of the salvage boat on the radio early, and we worked out a deal for travel time, on site rates, and stand by fees. Considering it would take the *Cleo* all day to get to Arrid Island from her home port to the North was a frightening commitment. But there was plenty to do in the meantime to keep my mind from worrying about how to pay the bill.

We had a ten A.M. appointment with our airlifted load of supplies. The plane was due and we had to get out on the bluff across the island to pick up the drop. Drop is the exactly the word. We were standing on the hill when the single engined plane made its first pass. On the second run the pilot opened the door and pushed two flour sacks out into the rainy sky. This adventure was getting more far out all the time.

Clive, Geoffrey, and I scrambled to get the first two as he passed again, dropping two more. With a wave of his wings he was gone and we were trudging in the muddy grass back to the house with our booty.

We spent the afternoon napping, reading, and waiting for the arrival of the *Cleo*. When they finally arrived it was completely dark. The crew appeared at the door with no warning from the dogs. They always barked when people came around. What an ominous beginning to the next strange chapter of our shipwreck experience.

And what a sight they were! A Hollywood casting director could have done no better if asked to provide modern day pirates for a sea going adventure story. Our Captain looked about thirty, tall and skinny with sunken eyes and pockmarked complexion, thin stringy brown hair, and a crooked smile of rotten and missing teeth to complete the grisly picture. He reeked of whiskey and diesel and looked as though he lived in the same clothes for weeks. It was going to be hard to have a lot of confidence in this fellow.

NEXT WE SAW THE CAPTAIN. WHAT A MESS! HIS EYES WERE GLAZED AND SQUINTING AGAINST THE LIGHT, THE PUPILS WERE JUST TINY DOTS. THERE WAS A DROOL OF VOMIT IN THE CORNER OF HIS MOUTH, RUNNING INTO THE ROUGH STUBBLE OF HIS UNSHAVEN FACE.

His mate was was much younger and cleaner but even less trustworthy looking. There was no innocence in those beady shifty eyes. He said almost nothing, but I had the feeling he was always looking around the room to see what might be good to steal.

After minimal discussion of the wreck and the location, the Captain got straight to business. Now that he was at Arrid Island his fees suddenly doubled. It was a take it or leave it offer. Of course we didn't have to pay, in which case they would simply raid the wreck without us!

We were also painfully aware of the fact we had no choice but to accept, since there was no other boat or crew available within a hundred miles. As curtly as the meeting began, it ended with our agreement to his terms. The plan was to begin the work at dawn the next day. When they left the house to head back out to the *Cleo*, Clive warned us to be on our guard, as if he had to anyway!

At first light, the crew of the *Seminole* was on the beach looking out at our "salvage vessel." What we saw further added to the movie-like character of events. *Cleo* turned out to be the oldest wooden fishing boat in New Zealand. Built before the turn of the century and showing her years in every way, her appearance gave us no more reason to be confident. Peeling paint, cracked rails, a continuous stream of bilge water pouring over the side from an old bit of garden hose, and a jumbled heap of gear on the stern deck, gave us the impression that she might soon be on the bottom too.

We were rowed out by a swarthy young Maori who looked a perfect match for the other pair. Once aboard, the four of us communicated with each other with glances of doubt and tried to make the best of the possibilities.

It was a short trip from the protection of the tight little bay around to the location of the wreck. It was relatively easy to spot the *Seminole* from the deck of the *Cleo*. Anchored so we were almost directly over our submerged former home, we began the preparations for the first dive. The fathometer reading to the bottom said sixty feet. This was going to force us to make every descent count because a diver should only spend one hour a day working at that depth before there was danger from the "bends."

I drew a "map" of the location of the valuables on board. Passports, traveler's checks, binoculars, tools, and anything else that would be easily convertible to cash were described. The mate checked out Iris on the spare wetsuits and gear but didn't wait for her. Instead he quickly slipped below the surface just enough ahead of her to raid the document case and hide the passports and money in his wetsuit. By the time Iris got down, the deed was done and would be denied until much later in the game.

On deck we felt the tugs on the lifting line and began the process of hoisting aboard all the loose gear that had good value. Quite quickly there were bags of sails, boxes of tools, anchors, chain, and coils of rope. Just about everything that was easily removable came up with the first dive. A half an hour put the mate and Iris back on board to tell us about the condition of the boat.

Iris described her as looking ready for sea. She was sitting on the bottom just like in the boatyard except sixty feet down. Resting on her keel, she was perfectly upright, with the anchor I set the night of the wreck dug into the soft, white, sandy bottom a few hundred feet away. Closer inspection revealed a half dozen or so football sized holes along the waterline, port and starboard, about midships. The mesh and rods of the hull structure were pretty much intact, but the concrete mortar was crumbled away. There was some minor damage to the rudder. Other than that, the hull was like new.

Inside was a different story. Besides being very dark, everything in the entire interior was all floating weightless in the gloom, making finding anything difficult. Iris had a hard time delivering the story without breaking down, like speaking of the loss of a friend.

While she and the mate rested, we plotted what else we could get out of the two remaining periods underwater. The diving was dangerous, cold work and we would have to use this time conservatively.

By the afternoon we had recovered a sizeable collection of gear. In deference to the tension and exhaustion of both crews, we headed back to the wool shed to store and wash down the tools.

Over dinner we began to discuss the possibility of saving the whole boat. The damage seemed to be repairable, even under water. We began throwing ideas around that might have had some possibility. We could float her with air bags or inner tubes, but had no idea where we might find some or how to actually do the job. Considering our location and the isolation, every idea we came up with sounded as hopeless as the last. Finally we agreed that removing the mast and boom would be the next day's project. There was no telling how long the good weather would hold. It had been calm for a day, but in New Zealand, even in summer, one can never be sure.

Sleep came easy that night for all of us, and dawn seemed earlier than usual. After a quick breakfast we were on the beach and ready for another day. There was no sign of life on the *Cleo*. We took Clive's little boat and rowed out to see what was going on. As we bumped alongside we were greeted by the mate crawling on his hands and knees out of the tiny wheelhouse. He looked to be in really bad shape. Hung over would be a kind description.

Next we saw the captain, our captain. What a mess! His eyes were glazed and squinting against the light, the pupils were just tiny dots. There was a drool of vomit in the corner of his mouth, running into the rough stubble of his unshaven face. He maintained his upright position in the forward hatch for a minute without saying a word, then unceremoniously puked on the deck.

I couldn't help but laugh as I looked over at Geoffrey and said "This is our captain? We're actually paying for this?"

It took the Maori crewman to tell us what had happened, since he was only hungover from whiskey and not in such a bad way. Seems the captain and his mate had swiped our medical kit on their way back to the boat and found the eight thirty milligram ampules of pure morphine. Now it was clear why our Captain looked so wasted! He was a junkie! Now he was a geezed out mess, probably lucky to be alive. Our departure would have to be delayed while our noble friend recovered from his dose.

The four of us began to make the *Cleo* shipshape for the day's work and to make sense out of what was going on. We were quite surprised to hear the drone of an aircraft overhead. After one pass over the bay, a small seaplane glided to a landing on the glassy surface. What was in store for us now?

On board the plane were David and Anthea Oliphant, (Lena's sister and brother-in-law), her father Andy Kerr, a friend of David's named Tony Sheppard, and of course, the pilot. They had only heard third hand reports of our situation and decided to come see for themselves what was happening.

David and Tony were avid divers and brought complete gear with them to help us in any way they could. They also brought a carton of cigarettes, chocolates, and four gallons of whiskey! They had a very interesting idea of the deprivation we were suffering, and certainly had no clue about the effect their gifts would have on our little group.

David and Tony came straight aboard the *Cleo* with their gear. Under the relatively calm hand of Maori Tom, we chugged around to the wreck site leaving the pilot, Andy, and Anthea to visit with Sarah. With nine aboard, *Cleo* had a full house.

David and Tony were an interesting combination. Drawn together by their common interest in diving, they were quite unlike in lifestyles. David was a prominent attorney and connoisseur of fine wine, while Tony was a rugged paving contractor who'd rather have a jug of beer. They were both there to help us, do some diving, and have some fun. In their wetsuits and diving gear, any differences disappeared.

It's a good thing they came, because the mate was in no shape to be underwater, and it was perfect conditions for diving. Now with three divers we stood a chance of making good progress.

First order of business was to secure the boat. They took the two anchors that remained on board and set them firmly in opposition to the anchor that was already out. This was done to attempt to prevent the boat from moving around should there be a surge from a swell.

Next they finished the job of removing anything easily disconnected. We hauled this stuff on board, then rested and ate lunch. The final project was to be the removal of the mast. This required the divers disconnecting all the standing and running rigging. A time consuming job on the surface, and more so in the half light sixty feet down, this would be the most serious challenge we faced so far.

The mast was a tapered box section Sitka spruce laminate that had taken six months to build. Complete with wires, boom, hardware, and sails it would have great worth. We were determined to get it loose from the boat and onto the beach. Time was running out before Tony and David had to get back to the seaplane and home to Auckland. When the job of loosening the rigging was done, we began lifting away with *Cleo's* ancient windlass. The spar just wouldn't budge. The soft cedar wedges around the deck partners must have swollen from the days under water. The mast was stuck like the sword in the stone. We strained the lifting gear until *Cleo's* deck was awash, and then the aged cargo boom broke with a crunch. Time had run out. The seaplane was powering around the corner. It was time to go.

Anthea and Andy were already aboard the little plane, and Lena rowed over to say goodbye to her dad and sister. David was enthused about the idea of actually saving the boat. He suggested I simply get aboard the plane and fly back to Auckland with them to try to set up something real. Dump the pirates and get some professional help.

Geoffrey and Iris went along with this saying they would take care of any remaining details of securing the boat and terminating the *Cleo* and her crew the next day. Almost before I knew what was happening I was in the plane, gliding over the smooth water, and lifting into the sky. The pilot gave us an aerial tour around the little island then headed West for the seventy five mile flight to Auckland.

From the moment of the wreck, the adventure had been non-stop. Rotten weather, insane hard work, airplanes dropping food, scurrilous scavengers, and now my very first ride in a seaplane! I was heading for the big city wearing the clothes of a man a foot shorter and fifty pounds heavier than me, without a single document of identification or even a dollar in my pocket. A quick trip to the Salvation Army station would take care of my clothing problem. The rest, we would see.

The evening found me settling into a little room in Lena's mother's house. Up the street from the Oliphant's, it was a cozy little place with a view of Auckland's harbor entrance. Fiona, Lena's sister, was living there at the time while their mother was in England on vacation. A pile of telephone books and a phone would be all I needed for the next few days in the search for a real salvage effort.

For the first half day I made call after call, trying every possible source of marine salvage and diving. Some of the people seemed interested, until I told them the boat was sixty feet down and seventy five miles offshore. I knew whatever happened it had to come together before the weather changed.

The first responses were all so negative I gave up early in the afternoon and called David and Tony with a desperate scheme. Could they get together a group of divers, a boat, and wrecking tools? We would go out to the island, a band of scavengers ourselves, and tear the *Seminole* apart underwater, and take what we could along with what had already been retrieved in the first day's diving. We would simply get out while it was still possible.

Tony was his enthusiastic self, agreeing with the idea. He said he thought he could have it together by the following evening. It was some sort of friendly magic. Out of nowhere there were trucks full of tools and diving gear, food, beer, and ten excited Kiwi guys ready for a crazy adventure.

Tony arranged to have the *Concorde*, a sleek fifty foot power launch, take us out to Arrid Island. The owner had lost a vessel of his own, felt some sympathy, and agreed to do it for fuel costs. We had spoken with Geoffrey during the morning network to say we were coming to get them and the salvaged gear. In order to make it happen quickly, they were going to have to get it all down closer to the beach and ready for pickup in the morning.

Lessons, lessons, a hundred lessons. Out on the island, my faithful friends labored through the afternoon, shifting all the cleaned and organized gear and tools the hundred meters or so down the hill from the wool shed to the corral on the beach. It was all bundled and ready for a quick dinghy ride out to the *Concorde*. With the job completed, the three of them went back to the house and got right into the whiskey again, happy they would be getting off the island soon. It was clear and calm as I FOUND MYSELF they walked up the trail in the early darkness, SCREAMING FROM unaware of the drama about to unfold. THE DEPTHS OF ME.

Clive and Sarah didn't have a stock of liquor normally, but he was finding it easy to sit down with the ladies and toss off a few whiskies before dinner. Sarah fumbled about in the tiny kitchen, now and then staring disapprovingly at the scene around her table. I'm sure she had never before seen her husband get so loose, or had to tolerate such behavior in her house. It was eating her up, even though it was only innocent playfulness. Those girls! And they were always sneaking off together to smoke cigarettes. This was truly not normal for Sarah.

Meanwhile I was enjoying the first few hours of smooth going on the *Concorde's* journey across the Colville Channel. This channel is easily one of the most rugged and unpredictable anywhere. The gang on board was having a fine old time, as if we were headed for a great party. But as we got into the more unprotected areas exposed to the North and East, the ground swell picked up and the wind increased steadily. Within the third hour, the wind was up to gale force and rain was beginning to fall. It soon became apparent that we had to turn back. The *Concorde* wasn't a heavy weather vessel. Disappointed, our party backed off and everyone dozed as we raced the deteriorating weather back into Auckland Harbor and the safety of the marina. We unloaded all the gear in the increasing rain, thanked everyone, and went home. Tony dropped me off at the house around one A.M. with the trees in the neighborhood waving wildly in the lamplit rain. I felt beaten, physically and emotionally.

THE SEA YIELDS ITS TREASURES UNWILLINGLY.

Lying in my bed I listened for a long while as the rain and wind increased. By three A.M. or so, it sounded as though the windows would rattle out of their frames. It was quite lucky the *Concorde* and her crew made it home safely. This was about to become the worst storm to hit New Zealand in fifty years!

The wind and sea built quickly out on tiny, exposed Arrid Island. While the crew slept, angry waves boiled into the little bay and took away all we had salvaged from the wreck, as well as the loading chutes and corral that were made from huge, rough hewn timber. Ten foot surf closed out the entrance to the bay and rolled all the way to the beach in a head high shorebreak.

In the morning, Lena got up with Sarah. It was a furious storm with giant wind gusts and blasts of dense rain. In a lull she hurried down to the beach to see what was going on, and was suprised to find there was nothing there to see. She went back in the house to find out where the others had put the stuff safely away, only to be told no one had touched a thing. It was all simply gone.

The rest bundled into what clothes they had, and together with Clive, struggled down the trail against the screaming gale. When they got there, they could see it was true. Gone. All gone.

Back in Lena's mom's house, Fiona and I could tell we were in for it big time. Trees were crashing down in the neighborhood, the power was out for hours at a time, and it was difficult to see more than a few blocks. The news was all about the closing of roads and the warnings to stay safe at home. The afternoon TV news had pictures of the toll plaza area of the Auckland Harbor Bridge littered with the wreckage of forty or fifty boats that had once been moored in the basin near the highway. All over New Zealand was carnage, and it wasn't going to get better for a few days.

That day was spent resting and planning. Phones were out of the question, and most businesses were closed. Fiona and I sat by the fire, and she let me ramble on with various schemes and acted like a foil for the crazy ideas, adding to some and dismissing others as a bit crazy. I felt guilty for not being on the island, but now there was simply no choice.

The next day I must have made a hundred phone calls. Conditions were still bad but the Kiwis are a hardy lot and most places were back at work. By trial and error I developed a plan. Ask fifty people what to do, get forty seven "You're crazy!'s", three decent suggestions, and the world opens up to you.

Filling the hull with ping pong balls was out, pumping her full of foam too. Inner tubes might have done it, but getting enough and getting them full was another problem. Finally a diver at a shop suggested we float her with drums of air, like a giant raft. This quickly progressed when he said he knew of two, used two-thousand gallon fuel tanks that were available.

I found a company who made an epoxy that cured underwater to patch the holes, started looking into a boat for the trip, and went to where the tanks were. David Oliphant floated the entire scheme on his credit, and before dark the tanks were moved on a trailer from the field where they sat for years, into the base yard of commercial diver, Captain Bill Kidd. No kidding. Billy Kidd.

That evening, Fiona and I made a nice dinner and talked about the others and what they must have been up to, as we hadn't heard anything from them in a few days. More time by the fireplace, more schemes and dreams, and then fitful sleep. It was still hard to believe in my new reality.

In the morning it was no trouble to get up and be excited about the day ahead. This was going to do it. I was confident and had a plan. The trip to Captain Kidd's was an opportunity to think and be ready for a long day of action. As soon as I got there he listened to my ideas and added a few of his own. We agreed the place to begin was inside the tanks, so I suited up and crawled in through the inspection port. In the darkness I could see every pin hole that would need to be welded over. With a box of toothpicks, I marked as many as I could find, then climbed out to begin welding.

It took a whole day to make the tanks hold pressure, which they would have to do to float the boat. I welded every hole and added valves and chain lugs for the final touch. Exhausted but satisfied after the grueling work, Kidd and I had a beer, made a schedule for the trip to the island, and started gathering a crew and finding a boat that could do the job.

Billy knew about a fellow named Ken who had a half finished fifty-four foot dive boat. The *Harold Hardy* was a hull, deck, and trunk cabin, but was completely without an interior. Down below was a big cavern except for the engine room and steering station. There was nothing that could get too messed up from a bunch of crazy divers banging around. But she had a powerful engine, a microwave, and a huge ice box which would hold a sufficient supply of beer and steaks to keep our crew of Kiwis happy.

Ken agreed to charter us the boat and go along as skipper. We made a plan to meet near a local park where the tanks could be launched and dinghy-towed out to hook up with

the *Harold Hardy*. With the new crew aboard we began the long trip across the dangerous channel that had driven us back before. It would take us until the next day to chug out to Arrid with the big sluggish things behind us.

When we got to Arrid the little bay was our first

stop. The wind was strong from the direction of the opening of the bay and we ran into the tight little spot hoping to make a big turn and get anchored. Unfortunately, the windage on the boat and the tanks was pulling us onto the beach, so we cut the tanks loose and let them blow on the sand. We could get them later.

ROCKS IN THE LIVING ROOM, AND NOW SEVENTY FEET DOWN.

The sea yields its treasures unwillingly. The three day storm of the previous week had taken its toll. The mast was broken completely away from the boat and was quickly captured and anchored safely. The boat had been shifted and pounded into deeper water. I knew before the divers went down she was gone. As I climbed down the trail we had earlier scaled to our safety and got to the small protected bay, I found the galley locker shelves and pieces of the toe rails in among the rocks. I knew those pieces like they were my own bones. Geoffrey was more optimistic, but I knew right then our efforts could no longer save her.

Suddenly the game changed. One diver told us what we already knew. The port side was now unfit to cage chickens. Rocks in the living room, and now seventy feet down. The only hope was some sort of stripping operation to get the "jewelry" that was going to pay the astronomical hire rates. We were unprepared to deal with that. The whole of our energy of preparation had been put into saving the *Seminole*, not into dissecting her. A radio call arranged a plane to fly to Great Barrier. An air powered chain saw was soon in our hands. That's right ... a chain saw. For myself, I didn't want it... didn't want to hack the lovely lady to bits for money. It was small change after all the years, but I needed now to try and recover something.

So I stood and watched and helped. The crew who loved the *Seminole* so dearly saw it begin to happen. I could feel the teeth of the terrible machine tearing into the carefully chosen and lovingly worked wood. If it had been for me alone, I think I would have left her to rest whole to avoid the pain. Soon huge pieces of the decks and combings were coming to the surface, all with glistening bronze hardware attached. The first day was a rough one for all as the wind was up from the NW, making the bay we were in have big swells and chop. The pro divers were finding it very difficult to chop the 'Nole to pieces. Built it too strong, we did. By afternoon we had the cockpit area apart and the coachroof loose. The whole of the next day, the 28th , was spent trying to tear the main cabin top loose. Pulling with one inch rope and a twenty-five ton launch wouldn't budge it, even through it had been sawed almost completely free. Too many through-bolts and fasteners I guess.

About 3:30 P.M. on Friday afternoon, the cabin top came loose. We towed it to the beach in a squally rainstorm to strip the hardware. The mast stuck out of the top and bottom, still firmly wedged. I stood on the beach with a chain saw, in the rain and waves and sand, sawing that once beautiful thing to save fifty dollars worth of hardware. A few hours worth of dinghy trips to load the salvaged gear and our few possessions, and it was done. Goodbye to Arrid Island. We steamed out in much the same conditions we arrived; strong wind, rain, and almost no visibility.

In the midst of all the drama, we met the Constable of Great Barrier Island and in his presence, had a high seas meeting with the pirates, rowing over to receive all our traveller's checks and passports from them.

Our Arrid Island host, Clive, had injured his back wrestling the huge timbers in the storm and was air lifted by helicopter as we were preparing our own departure. The island's owner showed up in a large workboat to take Clive's wife, Sarah, back to Auckland, regardless of her protests. They left never to return.

It was dark, cold, and forbidding, powering along with the bones and organs of our departed friend aboard. All of us were exhausted physically, emotionally, and spiritually from our week long ordeal. It was odd to hear the *Harold Hardy's* sonar beeping to guide us when we couldn't see anything. It was too rough to continue to Auckland so we stopped in Great Barrier Island where we were put up for the night in the summer house of some friends of Ken's, the owner of *Harold Hardy*.

After a rest, some fuel, food, and beer for the divers and crew, then we were on our way again, arriving in Auckland on the evening of Saturday the 29th. On Sunday morning, my thirty-second birthday, everyone who had

assisted up to that point came to Stanley Wharf and helped unload. It was over for awhile. In the evening, the crew of the *Seminole* and the Oliphant family had a quiet dinner at David's home. Considering the circumstances, we still managed a lot of smiles. No matter what else, we could still celebrate the fact there were four of us on the rock that dark stormy night twenty days before. We never did lose sight of it.

Then we faced the business end. None of us had papers. Geoffrey and Lena recovered their soggy passports, but Iris and I were without. New Zealand immigration was very human for a change, granting us a one month visa, and customs even better. They didn't want to know about the salvaged gear. The man behind the desk owned his own boat and I could feel his understanding of the situation. The only bad vibes we got was from the American consul. Bureaucrats to the end, by the book, cold, behind bullet proof glass. Never in our passport dealings with the functionaires did we ever touch a hand in greeting or meet anyone without a protective window in between, although this did change later when the Consul General, a very nice woman, finally came to my aid. Then we had passports again and were legally in NZ.

Now for the part that will perhaps be the most interesting to my sailing friends. There is no way I could relate with words the day I ran to the top of the hill in the rain and wind to look down on the bay where the boat was resting. I found myself screaming from the depths of me, and everywhere I looked was raw, rugged beauty. Rainbows, sun through the grey clouds, rich green hills, and the sea, the sea. Mother Ocean is so indiscriminate, so gentle to us, yet so hard on our "things". For no matter what, we were spat out and deposited on the beach like seeds squeezed out of a lemon.

And our mistakes? We were loose from living on the hard. We all knew what to do but failed to in the little bits that mattered. We turned to run away from land but too late, already behind the tiny spot on the chart. Twenty miles of "maybe" sea room in a fifty knot gale on a lee shore is not enough. Although we were all experienced, we were not all versed in the overboard survival and engine drills. Iris didn't know how to start the motor; Lena didn't understand the Avon, and on and on, a thousand small things that might have made the difference.

The survival gear. We had a nine foot Avon dinghy with two gate valve type CO2 bottles for inflation. Once we realized we had to save ourselves and the boat was gone, I wasn't able to get the raft clear of the boat and inflated before it was pulled from my hands as she went down. It's clear to me now some type of near instant to automatic device is necessary to survive a sinking. The excellent survival valise we had prepared (it was full of everything we would need) went down with the boat, still lashed on. So did the overboard gear and strobe light, tangled with the boat. It happened so fast that we were swimming. I suppose if we considered ourselves first, and not the boat, we probably would have gotten it all together.

I learned how to deal with changes over the wandering years and found it not all that different. Breathe in, breathe out. The total expenses for the attempted salvage were near to the value of the salvaged gear. It would have been a good investment if the boat was saved, but not so good as it turned out. A few weeks of hard work cleaning the parts of sand and seawater got the gear in order for selling it.

All of us who have a fine ship or have built one may understand this, especially if it is all you have and it's worth a great deal of money. First, never put faith or trust into the boat. It is a thing. No matter how much soul or love it may appear to contain, it does not have a mind. Put faith in your crew, your friends, and yourself. Center it. When it's time to change something, do it. Our creations may be beautiful, functional, non-corrosive, and still sit on the bottom, for they cannot think. Mindlessly, they can make your day go from sun to grey.

As we all stood on the beach at Arrid Island, looking at the mountains and pastures, and the cozy house, we all had smiles for each other because we four will always know a few things about life and death that words do not fit. I may never get over being alive.

This little story wouldn't be complete without following through on my experience in the little Oriental shop. After getting everything completely squared away, working off all the debts, selling all the gear, I had to go back and see the fellow who stood out so clearly in my mind. I had to do it.

Lena went with me. We walked in together, the tiny bell announcing us. The little Chinese fellow looked up to recognize us and seemed surprised. Face to face I said, "I need to ask you something. Do you remember me coming in here about a month ago?"

He replied, "Yes. I do remember."

I responded, "I need to ask you a question. When I was here, did you put a curse on me?"

This didn't seem to faze him. He answered without hesitation, "Of course."

At that point I wanted to ask him a stream of questions but he spoke quietly, "Please come away from my customers, I have a private place we can speak."

I accompanied him through an opening that was covered by a gray canvas into a small room filled with more strange things. He turned and faced me, a complete contrast to me. He was small and slight, much younger than I, and certainly seemed no threat. We began a conversation that affected me all of my life going forward.

Our exchange began with me relating briefly what had happened to us and the boat. I finished my tale by suggesting if he knew he was somehow powerful, he had surely succeeded in humbling me completely. I also offered that if he didn't know he was powerful, perhaps he should watch his thoughts when it came to cursing people.

Without much emotion he explained he had been seriously into Magic, the Black kind. He was involved with a group of people who were practicing and playing around with the occult ideas of teachers like Alister Crowley. In fact, some of his fellow participants had their own bad experiences.

He took my hands and told me he had no idea he could have affected my life with a simple curse, a curse he had thrown out because he was so angry with my attitude and failure to recognize the situation and what it meant to him. Then I was carefully told exactly what to do to make sure there would never be any future repercussions from the curse (which I have faithfully done).

Standing in his strange space I could only find forgiveness and love. What was done was done and there was no going back. With his hands still in mine, I told him I had no anger anymore, nor any fear. It was enough to know that what I had been thinking wasn't so crazy after all.

Then he said something that stuck hard.

"Now you know that I have been into these strange things. I want you to understand that in doing all this I have been looking for something. But now I'm sure that you found it."

With that he let go of my hands and spun around to walk out through the gray cloth covered entrance, leaving me standing alone in his space. When I walked out, he wouldn't acknowledge me. Lena was relieved to see me, and after failing another attempt to connect with him, we went to the door, and passed through, the little jingling bell ringing us out. I have to admit, it was the best I felt in months.

Then it was time to get set for the next part of the voyage.

Like a bird without wings

A seaman without a boat

Is ready prey

For all the pitfalls and complications

The land has to offer.

He is a fish out of water

A candle with no flame

Banished to the world of landsmen

Never quite being part

Of what they think should be.

He only longs for

The rhythms of sea days

And the life out there

For those who haven't known

Some of her moods and mysteries

The oceans remain alien

Separate.

For that boatless seaman

It is all as if a dream,

And he cries

And keeps trying

To be out there

Again.

A new era for me.
It's all new and I'm stoked.
Play it by ear from here.

Dear Mom,

I sure do appreciate hearing from you so often. It's good to hear the news of old friends. I also appreciate the efforts to create a copy of the letter I wrote. I would also like to have a copy so I might finish an article I'm writing for money. Some of the letter I felt read quite well and I'd like to use it. Unfortunately, I have no copy.

I've heard from Claude. She wrote a beautiful letter, resigned further claim, and bid a farewell of sorts. I hope I'm in a position someday to do something to show her what she has meant as a friend and lover. She's always a very giving person and I hold her in high esteem.

Next week Lena and I will be heading north to make two Sioux Indian tipi's that are to be used as summer dwellings on Michael Morehart's land in Opua, Bay of Islands. He's presently building a one hundred and twelve foot sailing cargo yacht, the *Manutea*. There is every possibility an organization will be formed called **Commercial Sail Associates** to build sails for commercial sailing ships.

A new dream forming up. It can happen as soon as the loose ends from the last one are cleared away. Agonizing ties to the past won't bring some financial stability. This job will bring some in to support us. I have my bond covered now so I can get a visa extension to allow the completion of the sale of the hardware. When it's gone we'll go to Tahiti for a couple months and then to Hawaii. Maybe.

My life has taken enough strange turns in the last days and weeks I can't really predict or plan anything. I'm much more interested in doing what's happening now. Much easier to live with. Who knows. I may spend the stash on material for a new boat and split again. I figure though the thing that draws me to a scene should be listened to. I'm following in my own footsteps. An awareness of self like never before. I can't bullshit me anymore. It's really quite a mindblower sometimes. A quiet merry madness all my own. It's even a little frightening to feel the power we have locked in our will. No wonder some men lose control and become mad for it. Dynamism like that is always so within reach. It's only our lack of willpower that keeps us from moving mountains and flying. Every time we give in to the non-doing impulse, strength and power are drained away.

A huge psychic drain in the end, the excuses, envy, and doubt, scatter our energies and we can't concentrate them into effective power. God, what raving.

A new era for me. It's all new and I'm stoked. Play it by ear from here.

We must be going somewhere, there's no footprints.

Lena's mother is now in England staying with her mother. She's going to be returning to NZ around the end of October and could pass through S.F. If you'd like to communicate with her, she's been given your address, and from the things I hear of her, you may have a good time together. You may hear from her.

Thank you again for the correspondence. After all, it's much like talking, isn't it? May see you sooner than you think, life's so changeable.

Love,

Sticks

August 28, 1978
Auckland, NZ

Dear Grandma,

Wrap the blanket of love around your old strong shoulders and live in the light of friends and neighbors. Grandfather has been released from his frail useless body and his spirit will be resting in the gentle space between lives. He shall always be there in my heart. I can see him any time I wish. Even in this last year, he's never been farther away than a thought. You both live in visions and dreams. Yesterday only seems a breath away.

I wish you can still live your life in its fullest measure. I'm sure Ernie and Maria Rosa will help you out. It makes such a difference when you have people close to you.

The loss of the *Seminole* was like losing a friend taken before "his time". We all live with death as close as the next breath. I found that living is a unique opportunity. I will never miss the *Seminole*. She is with me always, as long as I live.

It's sad we can't sit together quietly for a while. Picking berries down on the riverbank, the warm sweet summer smell in the kitchen, cherries, berries, applesauce, so simple the good things we always did together. The bread. I'm not little Barry anymore except in my heart where I know you are now.

Perhaps in your life I shall see you again. It will be good.

Love,

Barry

Grandma,

On the eve.

I say to you

Because it must be.

Your man of

Nearly sixty four years

Is gone.

I honored his

Passing with my tears.

I loved him

As well.

Barry

BARRY SPANIER

September 10, 1978
Rainbow's End, Opua

Dear Mom,

Today is our last day on the farm. For a whole week we've been treated to sunny spring weather, but this morning it is grey and wet. This place is quite beautiful, glowing green trees everywhere. The house is very old, restored to bare wood beauty, and the folks who live here are improving it each day. Electricity is produced by wind power, and water comes only from the rain. Fruit trees are all around and their garden glows with love. Wardy and Erica are from Santa Barbara. He's building several versions of a very efficient wind generator, primarily for boats, but good enough for a remote residence as well.

The farm is owned by Michael Morehart, the American who is building the big sailing ship. We just finished building two Sioux Indian tipi's for him to be used as summer dwellings on the farm. They turned out quite well and should be strong and dry, at least for the summer weather anyway. The tipi is quite an ingenious structure, providing shelter in all weather for generations, without scarring the environment. Perhaps for the good of the planet, man should never have left the nomad stage.

This afternoon, we'll return to Auckland and the pace of city life. Lena and I plan to leave for Tahiti in two weeks. We both have tickets and are ready to go. I still have some gear to sell but I think it will all work out. What doesn't get sold, I'll either give away or ship to Hawaii to be sold there. My tools, sewing machine, and a few odd things will go. Not much really.

I'd like to stay in Tahiti for a month or more to draw a sail plan for Michael's boat, design some hardware, and do a little writing. I want to complete a couple of articles and finish the Reader's Digest story. I hope to stay with Patrick, possibly at the yellow house on Tahiti Iti. Lena and I are studying Tahitian together so we should have some knowledge of it by the time we arrive. Hawaii should happen around the end of November. It is a faith thing that brings me to Lahaina to build this new life. I feel it will be a sure happening thing.

Until September 22, I will use Oliphant's as an address. After that, I'll let you know. There is really nothing you can do for me right now. Lena's birthday is November 15th. She's 5'7", 37-29-36, long legs, long auburn hair and brown eyes. We're having a good time together working and playing. She'll be twenty-two soon.

I'll sign off now and write once before I leave. Thanks for sending a copy of the tale. Give my love to Grandma and tell her to write. I sent her a nice letter.

Love,

Sticks

We must be going somewhere, there's no footprints.

The lagoon is thirty meters or so from the deck, a nice lawn with palms and ironwood trees.

Dear Mom,

I'm lying here in the early morning coolness listening to the sea on the reef and the birds in the palms. We arrived in Tahiti on Friday morning, stepping off the airplane into the warm, moist, sweet-smelling air like nowhere else I know. Joel, Moea, and Patrick picked us up at the airport. How nice to be greeted by smiling faces.

Our present house is thirty-nine kilometers from Papeete, easily far enough away to help us keep our monies intact for a while. Two quick trips to town and 10,000 CPF are gone – voila. The house is a room, about twenty feet by twenty feet, bare floor, two foot high bamboo 'walls', and a fine pandanus roof. There is a nice deck on the seaside and a small adjoining shower and toilet room, also bamboo construction.

The lagoon is thirty meters or so from the deck, a nice lawn with palms and ironwood trees in between. The other side is a rich garden scene with palms, nice flowers and orchids everywhere, and large lawn area. There is much we can do in exchange for living here; building, lawn mowing, gardening, always something to do to keep the growing things in good order and the mosquito population under control.

I haven't begun my boat project yet. I want to get the house more comfortable. Need to finish some walls, build a table, and finish the roof on the shower. None of this is necessary to be able to live here, but it does pay the rent. When we get settled, we can use this as a home base to travel around more, and I can concentrate on writing and drawing what I must. Looking forward to hearing from you. I'm truly happy again.

Love,

Barry

November 7, 1978
Tahiti

Dear Mom,

Leaving Tahiti this a.m. on a Cal 39, *Galadriel*, bound for Honolulu. Should be eighteen to twenty-two days. Perhaps I'll phone on arrival, I'll write for sure. Should be a good trip this time of year.

Leaving Tahiti is always so hard with so many friends here. No time for a letter today, the Captain is in a hurry. Give my love to all.

Barry

This time we will make it!!

I may never get over being alive.

Freedom is having no concern
for how you're going to get from one day
to the next without status, money,
property, or possessions.

TAHITI TO MAUI

BARRY SPANIER

Nov 7 to Dec 15th
Tahiti to Maui

Lena and I were pretty much at peace with returning to Tahiti and being able to live in the little shack out in the country that belonged to Joel and Moea. Each day was an adventure and we never wanted for anything except the death of the diesel generator that ran each evening so the French political officer who lived next door could listen to the news until late at night. We would lay and plot how to disable it without getting caught, but the guy had a huge German Shepherd who would raise an alarm if you even went near their property.

After months of this generally simple and easy life we needed to think about how to get off the island before our visas expired. Once again, the universe arranged everything and provided us with the perfect solution.

Patrick had been asked by a friend about getting some sails fixed for a visiting Canadian sailor. He made the arrangement for us to meet Charles Priester, the owner of the *Galadriel*, a Cal 39 sloop. He had been out for about a year and was nursing some old headsails and wanted another row of reef points before heading north. And Patrick had a sewing machine... that didn't work.

So one afternoon, Patrick came in the old pickup and got us from the jungle house. *Galadriel* was anchored not far from where we lived and Charles was already in the truck with his sails. I wondered what he was thinking as we drove off to the remote house where we would do the work. Who were these people?

But by the end of the evening we were discussing getting on board and helping to sail *Galadriel* back to Hawaii. It made perfect sense to trade my work for passage, we would bring our own food, the rest was easy.

Within two weeks we were getting ready to go. Lena and I had connections all over for food. We picked green tomatoes and packed them in newspaper, same for green papayas. There were cabbages, taro, onions, and carrots from a local garden. When it was the day to go, our Tahitian families all showed up with even more; sacks of drinking nuts, bunches of bananas, a sack of rice, dried fish, and lots of fresh salad for the first days. They were all sad and crying that we were leaving. Charles was stunned with the load of food we put on the boat. He had only freeze dried camping food in three flavors, canned Spam, and those little Vienna sausages. We weren't going to live on that for three weeks or more.

The fourth crewman was a young French musician who spoke almost no English and was simply looking for a ride to Hawaii. That made it natural for Lena and I to be on watch together as Charles spoke French, but neither of us did. The challenges of language are always interesting and I expected to have a few before we got to the next stop.

When we left, the wind pattern was absolutely contrary to normal. It was November and the trades had gone somewhere else. The sea was smooth and oily looking and the heat was oppressive. The lack of wind prompted the use of the engine because Charles had an obligation to return the boat as soon as possible. His ex-wife was after her share. We charged on, burning fuel without worrying about the rest of the voyage.

After a little confusion about where we were, we had to resolve some issues about the basic navigation. I was keeping my own log and looking at the charts and **Sailing Directions** and sensed something was not correct when we spotted an island in a place where it wasn't supposed to be. No GPS in those days to help you out. Understandably, Charles wasn't excited about taking the advice of a recently shipwrecked crew member, but eventually with the aid of Chapman's book on seamanship, I was able to demonstrate that we had been treating the compass correction for variation incorrectly and were about twenty-two degrees off course. In fact it was a different island. Now we could take simple bearings to locate ourselves, and armed with the correct compass course, plotted a new line for home. The situation had resolved itself and a bit of breeze made us into a sailboat again.

This breeze was definitely odd though. Where we should have been almost close hauled on starboard tack, instead we were doing the same on port tack. This held all the way through the danger zone of the Tuamotus until we were free of the risk and in the safe open water.

As we charged along making good time, the attributes of a light displacement boat really paid off. We could sail efficiently in the lightest wind as long as we were willing to work the boat and change sails. My experience with sail trim allowed Lena and I to almost never have to power, while Charles' watch would often quickly lead to downing the sails and firing up the diesel. Fuel was burning much too fast.

Then things started to break. First a wire in the rig began to unravel from a broken strand. There were cable clamps and a reasonable collection of tools so this was just a simple jury rig with some other wire to bridge the failure. This was the beginning of a series of little things that kept us busy and prompted a trip aloft to inspect the rest.

Just before we got to the equator the wind did a complete swing to the dead south and soon we were running perfectly downwind with the spinnaker set and nothing else. The boat handled this so nicely it was almost funny. It was as if this voyage was going to give us everything one dreams of to make getting from Tahiti to Hawaii easy.

We had fallen into a relaxed routine and the earlier tensions disappeared with the easy sailing. I would make some hot chocolate or tea at the change of the night watch and stay on deck to talk about life and philosophy and relate some of my own choices. Sitting in the starlight and sharing ideas made the hours drift by and developed a common ground between Charles and I that wasn't there before. A year later, Charles made a trip to Maui and related to me that before his trip his classes were under-subscribed and not well attended. After he added some of the concepts we had discussed about sustainability, asset based currencies, and the corruption of fractional reserve banking, his popularity as a lecturer went way up. He said he had waiting lists for his classes now. And only recently he told me those times in his life had changed and influenced him in ways he could have never predicted. He was genuinely grateful for the experience I think.

The remainder of the voyage was reasonably easy apart from the string of small breakdowns that continued to give us plenty to do. *Galadriel* had been on the road for long enough to need a lot of little things. We simply did whatever was needed. The cabin table broke from its base so we just put it away. The compass light failed so we used flashlights until they were running low and then we used a star. Fuel was almost gone for the last days so we became better and better at sailing the boat. Food was the biggest challenge, and towards the end we were down to eating the freeze dried stuff almost exclusively. Only the peaches and apples had any real appeal. The rest tasted like food and you could live on it. But that was about it.

There was just enough fuel saved to power us into the dockside at Alawai Harbor. Not more than the few hours it took us to put down the boat were Lena and I on the road with our little bags. She would be hiding out from immigration for the next six or seven years. I had a passport and would be OK. A short ride on the city bus took us to Keehi Lagoon, where we knew the *Lavengro* was hauled, getting ready to sail us back to Maui. Geoffrey would join us there too and enjoy the ride to our new home. Voyaging was going to be over for awhile, left to be dreams.

Dear Mom

MAUI

BARRY SPANIER

A fine Maui day

on the Hana Highway.

He was a smiling guy.

He looked like a working guy

So I picked him up.

He said he was going to Hana,

"Just tryin' to fit in."

I told him I picked him up because of his smile.

We talked story.

"You live here?" I asked.

"Yep... A year now."

"If you run into Sky,

say, 'Hello' from Barry".

He said, "How long you been here?"

"Thirty years."

I had to turn up Ulumalu.

He smiled again and said,

"Mahalo, bro. I just gotta fit in."

"Keep smilin'." I said.

"I got to. Right now that's all I have."

As he walked away,

he was still smiling.

I had to shout,

"Don't worry. That's all I had when I came here."

December 15, 1978
Makawao, Maui

Dear Mom,

I'm sitting in a beautiful cedar home up on the side of Mt. Haleakala, looking out over the rainbows, green meadows, and forests of this fine island. The prospect of working here and being established seems it will be good for the future. We've been spending a great deal of time talking business, rent, and space. We're going to try and secure a space, put out a lead for a place to live, and then fly to California for the holidays. We will probably fly into S.F. but one way or the other; I'll phone and let you know. It could possibly be after New Years, but I doubt it.

You asked me on the phone what I wanted for Christmas. I'd like Marianne (Lena) to have Christmas with our family, so I'm going to front her a ticket. We don't have much money, but there's enough to make it there and back here. The only thing I don't look forward to is telling "the story" so many times again.

I'm hoping to accomplish a great deal during the holidays on a little project for the future. It will require being around S.F. as much as possible for a few weeks. I need to use a good shop and the technological resources of a big city to develop this idea. Timing seems essential to success. Many seeds are planted, now is time to work hard so the garden will flourish by harvest time. I have had many holidays in the last years – now is the time for work.

MauiSails, 111 Hana Highway

See you soon,

Love,

Barry

237

Dear Mom,

Got the funds safely stashed in a corporate checking/savings account. Plan to put some of it to work soon, buying some interest in a few large companies. A few shares of stock in Matson Navigation.

Got the first sails back from Hong Kong built to our design. They look great. Testing begins today. We received full design credit on every sail. "Designed by Maui Sails – Hawaii". It feels as though we did a good thing. These sails have a quality look for production work.

All in all, life is good with every reason to be happy. Events lead to other events as if by design. I am grateful for the ability to help manifest the dreams of wind energy that we have. Sailing ships are becoming reality!

Hope your trip to Europe was all as good as your messages suggested. We may go again in January for a big boat show in Munich. Don't know about the weather that time of year. My wardrobe will require some changes. Last trip, I froze.

Maybe you'll be able to come here. Escape the S.F. winter for a few days.

Keep in touch. Give me a call. Many thanks.

Aloha

Barry

SPANIER & BOURNE · SAILMAKERS · 111 HANA HWY. · KAHULUI, HI (808) 877-7443

Dear Mom,

Got the funds safely stashed in a corporate checking/savings account. Plan to put some of it to work soon, buying some interest in a few large companies. A few shares of stock in Matson Navigation.

Got the first sails back from Hong Kong built to our design. They look great. Testing begins today. We received full design credit on every sail. **"Designed by MauiSails – Hawaii."** It feels as though we did a good thing. These sails have a quality look for production work.

All in all, life is good with every reason to be happy. Events lead to other events as if by design. I am grateful for the ability to help manifest the dreams of wind energy we have. Sailing ships are becoming a reality!

Hope your trip to Europe was all as good as your messages suggested. We may go again in January for a big boat show in Munich. Don't know about the weather that time of year. My wardrobe will require some changes. Last trip, I froze.

Maybe you'll be able to come here. Escape the S.F. winter for a few days. Keep in touch and give me a call. Many thanks.

Aloha,

Barry

BARRY SPANIER

Squid Ink Pasta & Baked Ahi with Shrimp & Mushroom

1⁄2 lb of fresh ahi steak 1 1⁄4 in thick
10 21-25 size raw shrimp
2 tbs yellow sweet pepper
6 clove garlic sliced thin lightly chopped
Small hot cayenne
2 tsp soy sauce
1 tsp Thai fish sauce
2 Tbs Sake
Light sunflower oil
3/4 cup mayonnaise
Dice mushrooms, garlic, and cayenne
Sweet pepper

Chop shrimps into thin slices.
Cook mushrooms, garlic, cayenne, sweet pepper in oil lightly.
Add Sake and soy about 1⁄2 way through.
Cook liquid almost away.
Add raw shrimp and cooked mixture to mayonnaise.
Make a thin bed of it –
Place fish on and cover with balance of mayonnaise mix.

Set oven preheat to 400 – 15 minutes.
Put fish dish to bake at 10 minutes. At 4 minutes go to 425, then 1 minute to HI broil.
It will nicely brown – fish should be rare and shrimps pink.
Serve on pasta with green salad and quick cooked asparagus.

Squid Ink pasta (Neo Di Seppia) cooks in 7-9 minutes.
Put pasta in boiling water.

Dear Mom,

If I had to say all the great things about you, it would take a book. You were there in my corner even when I was hallucinating on your face at two in the morning. You were always willing to let me store all my boat building junk in your garage, to have a safe haven, even though I surely was a huge disappointment regarding my education and future. You never gave up, and I always knew you had nothing but goodness and light for me.

As the years went on and I found myself stuck in far places with no money, you would manage a Western Union transfer to some obscure bank and I would have a hundred dollars to get me to the next country or island. You became free to travel and soon were away from home all the time. Now you are traveling almost as much as me!

And to be able to know and play with you on a regular basis, to hear your exciting stories of your adventures and social life, makes me one of the luckiest sons there ever has been. You are my treasure, my big love, my soul support through any trouble, and I can only say THANK YOU and ALL MY ALOHA.

Congratulations, Mom, on your 92nd year. Only eight more until the wild party we've been planning for so long. Just keep having fun and it will happen.

Love,

Barry

BARRY SPANIER

MY MOM....

Since the letters in this book appeared, thanks to my mother, Cornelia, I have been easily transported back to the adventures of those years. Just as with so many other things in my life she did for me, this was a quiet gesture I never knew about until recently, when she began cleaning out old papers and photographs. A Mother's love.

Mom grew up in the Depression, going to college at Oregon State University during the worst of it. When the war started, she got married to my father, Ed Spanier, and he was promptly shipped out two weeks later for the South Pacific theater and didn't return for three years. Ten months after he returned, I was born in July of 1946, the leading edge of the baby boomer wave.

My parents struggled to make a good life and Mom always worked to keep things together, working as an assistant to a corporate executive, and later assuming his position. When I left on the boat in 1974, she was fifty-nine, recently divorced, and just beginning to explore new things for herself. She always loved sailing on the ocean, and as soon as we got to Hawaii she came to visit and lived aboard the *Seminole*, tolerating our rough camping lifestyle (no electrics, no head, no refrigeration), and growing to love being around the sea even more.

After retiring at seventy-one, she began to work in her field as a consultant, which gave her a greater degree of freedom in both time and finances. Then her love of boats and sailing became the focus of her traveling and personal adventures. There were voyages all over the world, in the Med, Turkey, Costa Rica, Tahiti, and all on relatively small sailing yachts. When the years made getting around in the tight quarters difficult, she shifted to larger cruise ships, always preferring to be floating for her adventures. Even today at ninety-four, she is actively planning more trips to exotic places.

All through my life one thing has never failed me, and that is the love from my Mom. She saved me by sending Western Union funds to far away places, opened her home to my friends, and never failed to send encouraging words or valid criticisms to keep me on track. I am blessed to have her in my life.

THE SEA

When I was twenty, Claudette and I went to New Mexico to check out some folks who had fled California, showing us their wonderful life in the purple mountains majesty. Living there was incredibly cheap, with almost no people around, and it would have been possible to be quite independent without having a lot of money. However, there was something seriously missing for me. The ocean.

After my initial exposure to the floating life on board the *Fairweather*, I could never shake the desire to be involved with sailing and the sea. Then with my years of wandering the South Pacific, the feeling has never gone away. It has been submerged by the reality of a total financial wipeout, the struggle to make a small business work without capital backing, and day to day land life needs of family, children, house and garden.

Seventy five percent of the planet is wet. Sail across an ocean in a small boat and the vastness of it will stun you into the realization of our insignificance. All life on Earth is completely dependent on this watery covering. Yet most of humanity lives outside this recognition, never considering its importance to our survival or seeking much knowledge beyond superficial awareness. Bernard often referred to life in society on land as the Snakepit, and money as a cruel poison to the true spirit of man.

The sea is neither benign nor malignant. It simply is there. No emotion, no plans, it has no care for you. A life on the sea is one hundred percent unpredictable, literally from moment to moment. Things as simple as having a taste of pure clean water, something green to eat, being able to enjoy restful uninterrupted sleep, and simple human interaction, are not found out there. A person who chooses to live afloat should put their head on one hundred eighty degrees from normal and look from a fresh viewpoint.

Although I have lived the last thirty years on land, traveling the planet has been part of my life. Sailing on boats has always been available to me and appreciated, but I always had to return to 'normal' land living. I often found myself staring at the far horizon wishing the day sailing trip wouldn't end. My business travel destinations were mostly associated with water sports, and consequently I have been to most countries on all continents. However, when voyaging, the pace is humane, the challenges more direct, and the soul rewards deeper and more significant. Anyone with a credit card can hop from land to land, but living and prospering on the sea has little to do with credit.

The fifty percent of the time you are sailing that is sooooo good, makes up for the half that may be less than enjoyable. You must adapt and yield, leave schedules behind, live by seasons, not dates, and be ready for just about anything. And I know there is still a dream to be followed, a dream to be out there again. Soon.

APPENDIX

Sailing ships are powered by an energy source that is free of direct cost, political control, and pollution, and is available in effectively unlimited supply.

Escalating oil prices will continue, and costly "efficiency" improvements on existing cargo delivery systems will never result in stabilized costs for us, the users of the service, as long as ships burn oil.

COMMERCIAL SAIL ASSOCIATES

CSA

In 1980, Spanier & Bourne Sailmakers business was making heavy duty charter boat and yacht sails, rugged and tough enough to handle serious daily use in the harsh conditions of the Hawaiian trade winds. All this work on these big boats and the history of working with large vessels of all kinds drove my interest in promoting the idea of manifesting the return of sail power to our merchant fleet. I registered a company called **Commercial Sail Associates** with the idea of working as a consultant for the sails and rigs of craft such as imagined.

This effort began with some well considered hand written letters to the senior Senator from Hawaii, 'Sparky' Matsunaga. He was very responsible and quickly returned the correspondence, beginning a long relationship by mail. His prompting motivated me to join up with a personal friend and librarian from Kahului, Jill Leveroni. Her enthusiasm and research expertise was really helpful, and together we created testimony and evidence to support our ideas.

Senator Matsunaga followed through admirably by supporting a Bill in the Senate (SB2992) that was delivered using our evidence as the basis for consideration. As is usual with most bills, it went nowhere, regardless of its quality or potential effect. But just getting the idea in front of Congress was a good beginning.

Now, thirty years later, I found these documents, and re-read them, finding them to be just as relevant as they were back then. To demonstrate that the concept was valid then as now, the whole communication, proposal, and bill have been resubmitted to President Obama, Senators Akaka, Inouye, Kerry, and Representative Pelosi for consideration. What follows is the recent complete submission and I think you will also find there is every reason to consider this as a meaningful way we could demonstrate to the world our total commitment to reducing carbon output, restoring American shipbuilding, utilizing our superior sailing technology, and putting a large number of souls back to work again.

AMERICAN SAIL POWERED MERCHANT FLEET

ALTERNATIVE PROPULSION & ENERGY SYSTEMS PROPOSAL AND SENATE BILL S2992

1978 - 1980

BARRY SPANIER

LETTER TO U.S. SENATOR HAWAII SPARK MATSUNGA
TRANSCRIBED FROM HANDWRITTEN

April 1979

Dear Sir,

I think it's time to stop and think about oil, the ocean and the wind.

Generally one would conjure up some picture of a shiny black slick being blown upon some shore following a shipping catastrophe. I see something very different. I see wings of white oil, transforming the endless currents of the ocean of our atmosphere into silent clean power, moving goods and people all over the earth.

Humans have such self-serving memories that they cannot reach back even forty years to a time when there were still lumbering, heavily rigged, undermanned sailing vessels with natural fiber sails competing on an open market with steam and oil powered ships. And that was when bunker fuel cost $1.30 a barrel! What has happened to the true seafaring tradition of the American nation? We are in an oil crisis, or so we are told, and still there is no move to return to sail as an alternative. All we seem to get instead is rotund financiers speaking of nuclear fuel as the only alternative. What of those dangers? Oil spills will be nothing compared to nuclear ships colliding, grounding, breaking up, and melting down. No thanks!

A sailing ship travels without a trace (except cooks garbage to feed a hungry crew that have probably worked up an appetite) and it can do it again and again on the same original "oil investment." Out of all the oil consumed in the U.S., only 1% is used to produce synthetic fibers. What small portion would be needed to produce the fabrics and cordage to operate fleets for many years! How many barrels would we save every time an ocean was crossed with the wind for fuel?

GO WITH WHAT YOU GOT

Too much work? I say yes and no. Perhaps a man (or woman) would have to stand a night watch and handle sails and lines but it will make them strong and healthy. Need jobs for people without jobs – convert the merchant marine to sail. Don't laugh at it. Think about it. As my representatives, I want you to speak for me in this regard. The sooner the work begins, the richer we all shall be for it. We have the broadest technological base and have long been the best sailors on the planet. Let's take advantage of these facts and be first with the fastest most efficient sailing fleet that can happen. Those who are first with the best seldom follow. Let's haul that grain to the Saudi's using our own oil in an economical and environmentally conscientious manner.

I would appreciate a response to this letter to get your views on this matter.

Yours very truly,

Barry Spanier

Spanier & Bourne Sailmakers
111 Hana Highway
Kahului, Hawaii 96732

BARRY SPANIER

SPARK M. MATSUNAGA
HAWAII

WASHINGTON OFFICE:
362 RUSSELL BUILDING
WASHINGTON, D.C. 20510

HONOLULU OFFICE:
3104 PRINCE KUHIO BUILDING
HONOLULU, HAWAII 96850

CHIEF DEPUTY
MAJORITY WHIP

CHAIRMAN, SUBCOMMITTEE ON
TOURISM AND SUGAR
COMMITTEE ON FINANCE

MEMBER:

COMMITTEE ON ENERGY AND
NATURAL RESOURCES

COMMITTEE ON
VETERANS' AFFAIRS

United States Senate

WASHINGTON, D.C. 20510

July 9, 1979

Mr. Barry Spanier
Spainer and Bourne Sailmakers
111 Hana Highway
Kahului, Hawaii 96732

Dear Barry:

Thank you for your eloquent letter concerning the use of sailing ships as a means of turning away from our heavy dependence upon oil as an energy source.

As you may know, I am a strong supporter of wind energy. There is no question in my mind that wind energy can make a substantial contribution to the United States' energy supply in the future. In Hawaii, where trade winds blow over 70% of the time at speeds of 17 to 24 miles per hour at windy parts of the islands, and where 92% of the time wind speeds are in excess of 9 miles per hour and sufficient to generate electricity, wind power could provide a major part of the State's electrical energy needs. With the continuing increase in the price of imported oil, and the adverse effect such imports have on our economy, the development of cost effective wind generated power approaches nearer by the day. And while public interest has thus far centered on the development of stationary windmills, the same circumstances should apply to the use of wind in powering ships. Thank you for bringing this possibility to my attention.

Again, I appreciate receiving your thoughtful views on this matter.

Aloha and best wishes.

Sincerely,

Spark Matsunaga
U.S. Senator

Alternative Propulsion and Energy Systems
Commercial Sail Associates
March 1980

In the years ahead, men will find it wise to utilize sources of energy that are presently lying dormant. Our dependence on fossil fuels for the transport of goods and people will soon become uneconomical, both in a financial sense and as regards the finite quality of natural resources. We support the common sense of alternatives, providing they don't use more resources and energy than they intend to save.

Our primary concern is the ship. At present, it is a fuel guzzler and can still move cargo relatively inexpensively. But with changing values effecting trade, the realization that resources have become more valuable than time, and the evolution of sailing ship technology, we will soon find sailing cargo and passenger carriers will be highly competitive economically and closely competitive in the same sense. And, don't forget the considerable savings in fossil fuels.

It is our desire to provide sails and sail hardware for the ships of the future as well as the ones that exist today. We allow that there are only one or two sail lofts in the world today that have the orientation necessary to provide a ship with sails that are serviceable in a commercial sense. Most lofts specialize in yachts, passing on the considerable expense of advertising and racing campaigns to the customer, all the while reducing labor time to maintain profits.

Only fifty years have passed since any significant number of large sailing vessels have been used commercially. It has been a lazy and shortsighted approach to the problems of pollution and energy waste that allows the internal combustion engine to continue to be used so willingly. The jet and the turbine are even worse. The power economics connected with huge capital investments have so little to do with nature or the quality of life on our small planet. Soon however, gracefully quiet vessels will ply the trade routes carrying goods and people across the seas, utilizing the power in the wind and leaving no trace but their wake.

This is not some antidiluvian dream, but a practical approach to a global problem. At least to one important aspect of it anyway. Ships such as these will have no rules to govern them except efficiency, function and sensible sea-keeping ability. There is room for newness in every respect and it is this newness that is our interest.

Do you have an idea? Perhaps there is a rig you want to try that is new, or maybe even very old. We have some fine young dynamic minds available who are unafraid to be unique and inventive. Does your ship have unusual sail requirements that a "yacht" loft might shy away from or attempt to discourage in lieu of something they are more familiar with? Should you have to pay for an international racing campaign and expensive advertisements to guarantee creative input on your behalf? Ships need sails for ships, not oversized yacht gear. Hardware and construction must be up to the job to be done.

Our gear will not be patented, nor trademarks registered for once again it is the customer that must pay for this legal service. We want to see ships sailing and to sail on them, not waste precious time and money protecting ideas that belong to all men. The law will not guarantee quality in workmanship or concern with your problems. We feel our products and services must be continually evolving to be the best obtainable, never living on a reputation, satisfying our desire to see a job well done.

Present projects include design consultation on a fifty net ton cargo schooner, two sailing fishing boats and small alternative ocean vehicles for individuals. Production of several interesting sail hardware designs is underway along with constant research into alternatives. Our new loft is constructed to serve the big ship first and provide the best service possible. We also provide a mobile loft and riggers service for emergency major repairs in out of the way places. Fee free to contact us for particulars.

Barry Spanier
Commercial Sail Associates
Maui, HI

THE WHITE HOUSE

WASHINGTON

June 25, 1980

Dear Mr. Spanier:

Thank you for your letter to President Carter. I apologize for the delay in replying; your correspondence came to my attention only today.

I am sorry you were dissatisfied with the handling of your previous letter. The large volume of mail received at the White House -- averaging some 40,000 messages a week -- occasionally necessitates a less detailed response than we would prefer.

We have noted your interest in emphasizing the use of sailing ships in the U.S. Merchant Marine as a means to conserve energy. President Carter shares your interest in using renewable sources of energy to lessen our dependence on petroleum products, an effort which will require the cooperation of all sectors of society.

We were pleased to have the opportunity to consider your proposal, and we are pleased also to send you our best wishes.

Sincerely,

Daniel M. Chew
Director of
Presidential Correspondence

Mr. Barry Spanier
Commercial Sail Associates
Post Office Box 1840
Kahului, HI 96732

96TH CONGRESS
2D SESSION
S. 2992

To authorize a study of sail-assisted technology as a means of reducing energy costs for inter-island transportation in the Trust Territory of the Pacific Islands, and for other purposes.

IN THE SENATE OF THE UNITED STATES

JULY 29 (legislative day, JUNE 12), 1980

Mr. MATSUNAGA introduced the following bill; which was read twice and referred to the Committee on Energy and Natural Resources

---

A BILL

To authorize a study of sail-assisted technology as a means of reducing energy costs for inter-island transportation in the Trust Territory of the Pacific Islands, and for other purposes.

1   *Be it enacted by the Senate and House of Representa-*
2 *tives of the United States of America in Congress assembled,*
3   SECTION 1. (a) The Congress finds that—
4   (1) The Trust Territory of the Pacific Islands is
5   composed of over two thousand islands scattered over
6   three million square miles of the North Pacific Ocean
7   with a total land area of only seven hundred square

2

1   miles supporting approximately one hundred thousand

2   persons;

3   (2) the health, safety, welfare, as well as the po-

4   litical, social, and economic development of the peoples

5   of the Trust Territory of the Pacific Islands are totally

6   dependent on the adequacy and regularity of inter-

7   island transportation;

8   (3) the principal form of inter-island transporta-

9   tion, especially for the outer islands is and will contin-

10   ue to be surface transportation;

11   (4) at present inter-island surface transportation is

12   completely dependent on uncertain supplies of increas-

13   ingly expensive imported fuel;

14   (5) recent developments in sail-assisted technology

15   offer the potential for alleviating the dependence of the

16   peoples of the Trust Territory of the Pacific Islands on

17   imported fuel for surface transportation, thereby im-

18   proving the capability for regular supply schedules to

19   the various islands, relieving the fiscal burden on local

20   governments caused by the costs of imported fuel, and

21   strengthening the base for political, social, and eco-

22   nomic development of the peoples of the Trust Terri-

23   tory of the Pacific Islands.

24   (b) In order to ascertain the potential for sail-assisted

25   technology for inter-island transportation in the Trust Terri-

3

1 tory of the Pacific Islands, the Secretary of the Interior is
2 directed to review the transportation needs of the Trust Ter-
3 ritory of the Pacific Islands and submit a report to the Con-
4 gress by October 1, 1981, on his findings and recommenda-
5 tions.

6 (c) In preparing his report, the Secretary of the Interior
7 shall consider, but is not limited to, frequency of services,
8 present and alternative routes, cargo delivery, operating
9 costs, port and docking availability and adequacy, and the
10 impact on energy costs of the use of a second generation of
11 inter-island field trip vessels using sail-assisted technology.
12 The report shall set forth a scientific analysis of the potential
13 applications of sail-assisted technology as a means of reduc-
14 ing energy costs for inter-island transportation including, but
15 not limited to, statistics on windspeed, direction, wave
16 heights and currents; possible design configurations and
17 specifications for sail-assisted vessels; cost estimates for con-
18 struction, financing, and operation; and such other informa-
19 tion as he deems appropriate to determine the feasibility of
20 sail-assisted technology for inter-island transportation.

21 (d) The Secretary is directed to consult with appropriate
22 representatives of the various local government units in the
23 Trust Territory of the Pacific Islands as well as the Secre-
24 tary of Transportation, the Secretary of Commerce, and the
25 Secretary of Defense in preparing the report.

TESTIMONY FOR THE RECORDS

OF THE OPEN HEARING OF

THE UNITED STATES SENATE COMMITTEE

ON ENERGY AND NATURAL RESOURCES

RE:

ENERGY SELF SUFFICIENCY IN THE PACIFIC BASIN AREA

Honolulu, Hawaii

July 10 & 11, 1980

Submitted by:

Barry Spanier & Jill Leveroni
Commercial Sail Associates
P.O. Box 1840
Kahului, Hawaii 96732
(808) 877-7443

BARRY SPANIER

Commercial Sail Associates

The Hawaiian Islands are developing as a center
of world trade. The Pacific Region will be the prime
focal point for U.S. trade well into the next century.
Trade across the Pacific exceeds that across the Atlantic
and has since 1975. An abundance of raw materials in
the Pacific Nations, their relative political stability,
and the opening of the People's Republic of China, are
all reasons to consider shipping and our merchant fleet
in this region as important to our energy conservation
programs.

It makes good sense economically, ecologically,
and politically, to develop a system of ocean transport
for the Pacific Region that is not dependent on the
consumption of fossil fuels.

Considering the vulnerability of the Hawaiian
Islands in the event of a shortage of oil, we must begin
to eliminate the need for oil as a direct fuel. Our
primary oil dependence in Hawaii is caused by our shipping
services. Any major disruption of oil supply will quickly
halt the flow of essential life support materials to the
islands. This situation must not continue, especially
since we have a solution at hand. That solution is to
begin _immediately_ to create a fleet of sailing vessels
capable of moving our cargo. Sailing ships are powered
by an energy source that is free of direct cost, political
control, and pollution, and in effectively unlimited supply.

GO WITH WHAT YOU GOT

The West Coast to Hawaii trade routes began with sailing ships and only 50 years ago these ships were still delivering cargo to the islands. Since that time, the general abandonment of sailing cargo vessels due to the availability of cheap fossil fuel resulted in a cessation of their development as well.

But the development of sail power in general has not stopped. The world of the private ship, particularly racing yachts, has provided improvements in design and materials for sails, hulls and rigging that cast a whole new light on the capabilities of sail power.

It is possible now to have large strong sails with half the weight for the same strength as canvas, with resistance to rot and chemical attack, and superior chafe resistance. All these factors bring us lower maintenance costs, less time lost in repairs, and faster sailing speeds.

Fifty years experience in aero- and hydro-dynamics has optimized sail plan and hull design combinations. Optimal routing is now a function of constant computer analysis based on satellite weather data and predictions. There is little guesswork in course planning with Satellite Navigation, Omega, and other sophisticated yet relatively inexpensive systems. Finally, there is the option of auxiliary power. Very low values of auxiliary power can

reduce the variance of voyage times significantly. Thus,
even when conservative engine use strategy is employed,
voyage time can be predictable as well as competitive
with fuel driven ships.

At present it requires only 1% of the oil consumed
in the U.S. each year to make all the synthetic fibers we
now produce. Dacron for cordage and cloth is a miniscule
part of this production. Matson Navigational Company
publicly allows that 30% of its current operations budget
is spent for fuel which is, of course, burned once and
lost forever. It is our proposal to use this same fuel
much more economically, to harness the free clean energy
of the wind.

We can begin by selecting cargos and ship designs
that most closely fit current economic parameters. There
will have to be compromises. It will be necessary to
concentrate on simplicity of operational systems, lightness,
and speed.

Simplicity of overall ship design will keep construction costs down and allow for lower operating costs.
Every system needed to operate the technologically updated
sailing ships already exist.

Speed will be the early obstacle to conversion
from fossil fuel, because in today's economic system,
time has become money. It will therefore be important
that these new ships be as fast as possible. Vessel

lightness, possible now due to continuous advances in construction materials, increases payload for a given sized ship while increasing speed. In the beginning we will consider only voluminous cargo; heavier cargos and the ships to haul them will come later.

The nearly obsolete oil burning fuel system that cargo ships use now requires $20,000,000 for cargo handling at either end and $80,000,000 ships to do the work. Although they may cross the ocean in 4-5 days, handling, warehousing and consolidation of loads increases the actual delivery time for surface goods to at least three times the actual crossing time.

By creating a fleet of smaller sailing vessels, we will ease warehousing and distribution problems and possibly allow single island service. Construction, rigging, and manning of new vessels will create thousands of new jobs in a revived industry, an industry that is now being killed by its dependence on oil.

As experience and developments increase, ever larger payloads and faster passages will be possible. For now, however, conversion to sail power is an immediately viable solution to problems created by burning oil and the sooner it begins, the more oil we will have for the future.

Bunker oil to power the free world's commercial fleet of ships over 1,000 deadweight tons accounts for

8% of total oil consumption. This amounts to 200,000,000 barrels a year. Even in the absence of crisis, a potential savings of this amount justifies substantial investment in converting to sailpower.

Studies done at the University of Michigan in 1974 indicated that when the value of oil was at $11.25 a barrel, sailing ships were only marginally competitive with oil burning ships. With today's cost of oil at three times that amount, it is time to re-examine this option. The University of Michigan report also stated that there were no technical problems associated with the development of sailing ships.

Perhaps a more important factor is the amount of energy required for a 25 year period: that is, a Net Energy Analysis. Based on conclusions from calculations in 1976, the average "cost" per year of a sail powered system, including the original investment, is 15% of the "cost" of a fuel powered ship ("cost" being the total amount of energy required).

Escalating oil prices will continue and costly "efficiency" improvements on existing cargo delivery systems will never result in stabilized costs for us, the users of the service, as long as ships burn oil. Patrick Grey of Matson Navigation publicly stated when asked about plans to reduce fuel consumption, that "We certainly aren't going to look to sail powered vessels in the future." Who will?

Surely if we take heed of our great maritime history as a nation, and utilize a technology in which we command a lead, we will soon be moving our cargos without burning oil.

This commitment would mean more work for people but there will be rewards to inspire them to be involved. A revived spirit of competition for fast passage, the challenges of seamanship that can happen only on sailing vessels, pride in accomplishment, and the feeling of participating in positive environmental change all will attract our youth to merchant marine service.

Within five years graceful quiet vessels could be plying the trade routes, carrying goods and people across the sea, utilizing the power in the wind and leaving no trace but their wake.

It is time to pursue this alternative. Sails are an elegant and technically feasible energy conversion system that is not presently being considered by government energy planners. The sailing fleet that serves the Hawaiian Islands will also serve as an example to the world of our ability to utilize an energy source that is universally available in a virtually inexhaustible supply.

#   #   #   #   #

BARRY SPANIER

Barry Spanier
Haiku, Maui HI
bspanier@maui.net

Monday, 23 March 2009

President Barack Obama
The White House
1600 Pennsylvania Avenue NW
Washington, DC 20500

Re: Potential for an American Sail Powered Merchant Fleet

Dear Mr President,

As I watch with interest your action to reduce our nation's deficit and find more efficient and cost effective ways to operate this wonderful country of ours, I felt you would be open to a Bill that was presented to the Senate almost thirty years ago, but unfortunately didn't proceed.

The attached documents provide a brief overview of what occurred in 1978-80. My early exchanges and responses with Senator Matsunaga of Hawaii are not fully represented as some of the documents were never copied or retained, however there is enough of the communication to show this project developed.

The language and intent is still 100% applicable to our current financial and ecological situation. A concerted effort to adapt sail power to our merchant fleet is a solution to many problems. A demonstration project as imagined would be quick to implement and will produce immediate results in terms of our country's commitment to positive change, reduction of oil use, and major job creation.

My personal interest is to help ensure we are achieving your objectives as outlined in your Energy and the Environment strategy:

"President Obama and Vice President Biden have a comprehensive plan to invest in alternative and renewable energy, end our addiction to foreign oil, address the global climate crisis and create millions of new jobs."

- Within 10 years save more oil than we currently import from the Middle East and Venezuela combined.
- Implement an economy-wide cap-and-trade program to reduce greenhouse gas emissions 80 percent by 2050.
- Increase Fuel Economy Standards.
- Deploy the Cheapest, Cleanest, Fastest Energy Source – Energy Efficiency.
- Make the U.S. a Leader on Climate Change.

There is a valuable opportunity in recreating a sailing merchant fleet. The technology is not far-fetched or imaginary. The cover page illustration is based on a very successful sailing system now in existence and well proven to work on vessels the size required to service small markets. In a short time it could be scaled up to do the same on major trade routes. Job creation and capital investment in a functional infrastructure will go hand in hand with achieving your other goals of improved sustainability.

Thank you for your time and consideration in this matter.

Kind regards,

Barry Spanier

Cc: US Hawaii Senator Daniel K. Inouye
         US Hawaii Senator Daniel K. Akaka

ABOUT THE AUTHOR

Barry Spanier is a Full Scale Model Experimentalist/Sailmaker/ (Sailing Speed Specialist). He has forty years experience in sailmaking having built hundreds of full scale proofs of theoretical concepts, and has used day-to-day, one-on-one testing regimes to bring concepts to reality.

When Barry arrived on Maui in December 1978, he had $52.00 to his name and a dream. He and his friend and partner, Geoffrey Bourne, hung up their shingle at 111 Hana Highway, and **Spanier & Bourne Sailmakers (MauiSails)** was realized. The company was created to make sails for yachts, but evolved as the new sport called windsurfing found Maui to be one of the best places in the world to practice it. Their business grew, and before long they had fifteen employees and were working around the clock.

So impressed with their work, Neil Pryde International Sailmakers joined forces with MauiSails from 1982-1998 and Barry assumed the role of a Product Designer, developing patented plastic part systems, and supporting ten time PWA World Champion Bjorn Dunkerbeck with custom made prototypes. He participated in sponsored efforts to establish new Sailing World Speed Records by Pascal Maka (1982), Fred Haywood (1983, 1984, 1985), Patti Whitcomb (1985), and Brigitte Gimenez (1989). **MauiSails** achieved the U.S. S.B.A. Small Business Person of the Year for Maui County 1993, and U.S. Chamber of Commerce Blue Chip Enterprise Award for 1994. Barry had extensive global travel, participating in the building of the Neil Pryde branded products machine, creating a world-wide network of valued associates.

From 1998 to 2004, Barry became Head Sail Designer for Gaastra Sails International, contributing wide ranging editorial content to trade magazines, and began administering an active forum without censoring or content control, a radical step to communicate directly with their customers.

In 1994, Barry decided to resurrect the trademark **MauiSails,** and along with two partners, formed a company called Synergy Sports. As Head Sail Designer for **MauiSails** (www.mauisails.com), Barry is responsible for design, product development, copy writing, and general operations.

Barry is Director of Cislunar Aerospace, Inc., a company involved in developing full scale methodology for doing Computational Fluid Dynamics (CFD) on 3D grids generated from multiple photographs taken from several angles at the same moment.

For the last ten years Barry has been working with Robert Masters and Dr. Richard Sword to create **www.lifehut.com**, a free source of audio visual psychology aimed at stress relief and personal improvement.

Barry is married, has three children, Zeppo, Destiny and Cutter, and is currently living in Maui.